Reproduction from the manuscript known as the Book of Kells is by courtesy of the Board of Trinity College Dublin.

ETERNAL GEOMATER

The Sexual Universe of

FINNEGANS WAKE

Margaret C. Solomon

Southern Illinois University Press

Carbondale and Edwardsville

Feffer & Simons, Inc.

London and Amsterdam

COPYRIGHT © 1969, *by Southern Illinois University Press*
All rights reserved
Printed in the United States of America
Designed by Andor Braun
Standard Book Number 8093–0392–2
Library of Congress Catalog Card Number 69–17107

INTRODUCTION

ADMIRERS of *Ulysses* and *A Portrait of the Artist as a Young Man,* who have eventually determined to attempt *Finnegans Wake* and have given up in despair after the first few pages, should remind themselves of some of the things they must have learned, from their reading of those earlier novels, about Joyce's method and about his announced intentions. A nice touch of ironic humor in Stephen's conversation with the dean of studies is lost, for instance, unless the reader can hold in his mind fragments of information from the early pages of *A Portrait* in which Simon Moonan is associated with the word "suck" and is involved in a homosexual incident discussed by the boys of Clongowes but only subconsciously understood by the child Stephen.[1] The dean of studies, with whose dull consciousness Stephen plays maliciously, concludes his piece of moral advice to the heretical university student:

> It may be uphill pedaling at first. Take Mr. Moonan. He was a long time before he got to the top. But he got there.
> —I may not have his talent, said Stephen quietly.
> —You never know, said the dean brightly. (p. 190)

Such assemblings of widely-dispersed elements are constantly required of Joyce's readers. In *Ulysses,* the process is the same, and the complexity has increased. One must collect and sort words, phrases, sense impressions and fragments of information which have certain "colors" or shades of colors—like the pieces of a jigsaw puzzle that will eventually compose a finished pattern. The reader's capacity for storing the bits and pieces in the compartments of his memory breaks down. He has to go back again and again to fill up holes where there has been a subtle cut between related shades. In *Finnegans Wake,* of course, a more subliminal process is operating. It does no good even to try consciously to sort and hold the words and fragments of words by which a person's sensibilities are bombarded in the opening pages of the book. The reader must put his trust in the power of his subconscious mind to register impulses of vaguely familiar linguistic and literary allusion. He is presented with a pile of language and is given no model to follow; his best bet is to read on until certain aggregates of repeated material begin to cling together so as to form basic constituents for the complex whole. Adaline Glasheen's brilliant analysis of "The Opening Paragraphs" of *Finnegans Wake*[2] is largely a work of hind-sight. The elements are far more easily identified once a person begins to see the intended shape of the finished product.

Joyce has always placed upon his readers demands which correspond to his own creative goals. The writer's original "epiphany" must be re-experienced by the reader of the short story; the maze of the labyrinth must be groped through alongside of the puzzled, weak-eyed Stephen, until the fear of making a mistake disappears; the frustrations of Ulysses-Bloom, in his attempts to find his way "home," have to be shared by the baffled reader. In *Finnegans Wake,* Joyce's intentions are more grandiose, and the reader must be willing to accept a slow enlightenment as "work in progress." From Stephen's comparatively mild statement, in *A Portrait,* that he is going to "forge in the smithy of my soul the uncreated conscience of my race" (p. 253), Joyce moves, in *Ulysses,* to a bolder assertion, implicit in the triumvirate of Bloom, Stephen and Molly. Stephen affirms his significance as "a conscious rational reagent between a micro- and a macrocosm ineluctably constructed upon the incertitude of the void."[3] Bloom meditates upon a bewildering

> universe of human serum constellated with red and white bodies, themselves universes of void space constellated with other bodies, each, in continuity, its universe of divisible component bodies of which each was again divisible in divisions of redivisible component bodies, dividends and divisors ever diminishing without actual division till, if the progress were carried far enough, nought nowhere was never reached. (p. 699)

Molly merely wishes "somebody would write me a love-letter . . . true or no it fills up your whole day and life always something to think about every moment and see it all around you like a new world" (p. 758). It is a new universe Joyce is creating in *Finnegans Wake*, one that will satisfy the longings of Stephen to be an artist-God, the new-science speculations of Bloom, and the propagating desires of the earth-mother, Molly. The reader must expect to find chaos on the first pages. All the materials for the creative act are there, and they are disturbingly familiar, since the new world is to be fashioned out of the smashed fragments of the old. As a matter of fact, it is "The seim anew" (215.23),[4] and the reader will become more and more confident of his ability to recognize familiar patterns as the universe takes shape, section by section. The command, "Let there be light," may not come soon enough to satisfy impatient readers, but it will come.

The present study proposes to illuminate some of the dark passages of *Finnegans Wake*. It would be foolish to try, in this multi-dimensioned novel-universe, to undertake an exegesis comprehensive enough to cover every level of meaning. Hence, the discussion will focus on the universe of the human body that interested Bloom so much—in particular, its sexual parts—for every facet of the book can be (and, in my opinion, should be) related to this microcosm. I believe that this very preoccupation with sex was Joyce's cosmic joke. Taking upon himself the role of a God engrossed in sex—and using all the religious myths and symbols of creation to perpetuate his joke—was one way of using his jesuitical training in an act of defiance, a way of flying by (*by means of*) one of those nets which Stephen, in *A Portrait*, declared were flung at an Irishman to hold him back from flight. "You have the cursed jesuit strain in you," says Buck Mulligan to Stephen (*Ulysses*, p. 8), "only it's injected the wrong way."

FINNEGANS WAKE is a funny book, and I do not wish to spoil the joke by over-sexplication. Nevertheless, my analytical re-readings—occasioned by a curiosity about the constant linguistic emphasis on sexual overtones—have led to a far greater understanding, on my part, of the reasons for the major symbols of the book: namely, the male and female sexual organs of the human body. It has been fascinating to watch these stylistic components of a newly-created universe expand and contract, turn inside out and shift dimensions—in the manner of an optical illusion—all at the will (sometimes perverse) of the god-like artist. The sexual symbolism of the novel is pertinent to all historical, religious, cultural and psychological human processes; it is particularly relevant to the opposition and occasional precarious unification of art and religion, as exemplified by the twins, Shem and Shaun.

Joyce's desire to reveal and, at the same time, his compulsion to conceal the sexual symbolism result in the scatological subtlety of a non-malicious practical joke; yet, behind the comedy there is still an earnest not-so-young man. Moreover, the fact that Joyce used people to stand for genitals, and geometrical symbols to stand for people, gives the entire novel such formal weight that any discussion of content apart from structure is impossible. The devious elaboration of the word itself, plus the fact of its circling back on itself from the end to the beginning of the book, gives meaning to the endless recurrence of countless lives that take off in all sorts of directions and yet end and begin the same over and over again. Joyce deals with triangles and squares, mathematical equations and logical and rational formalisms because he had to counter-balance a tendency toward near-maudlin sentimentalism—an Irish come-all-you sensibility—to mortify his senses, so to speak, as Stephen tried to do after the preacher had put the fear of hell in his soul. In *Finnegans Wake*, real banality of theme, a tremendous sense of family and history, deep religious inclinations (which are continually slapped down by impiety and derision), and a longing for identity—all of which are revealed in the sexual preoccupation—are hidden behind a strictly formal genius. The human paradox which is Joyce and which, in *Finnegans Wake*, he shows to be every man, cannot be wholly communicated except through form.

I hope Joycean critics will not be offended by my failure to mention, in many instances, the work others have done on particular passages. Scholarship on *Finnegans Wake* must progress through community labor, and I have been helped considerably by an exhaustive reading of all available critical material; however, the method I finally adopted was an attempt to read the text with fresh insight, turning to secondary material for assistance only when a problem concerning the language failed to yield to intense study, or when my own limited knowledge of mathematics and physics needed bolstering. I grant many other interpretations, so long as the ones I here present are taken into account as well. *Finnegans Wake* is a big book; its levels are multiple. I've tried to confine myself to one position, but the vistas on all sides still seem to stretch out to infinity.

Margaret C. Solomon

University of Hawaii
Fall, 1969

TABLE OF CONTENTS

ETERNAL GEOMATER

1

THREE TIMES IS A CHARM

1] *The Prankquean*

THE BIBLE begins with myth: first the creation story and then, when man has appeared on the scene, the myth most important to the human being in history: the fall of man. *Finnegans Wake* follows a similar pattern. Chapter One begins with a cyclical image—"riverrun . . . brings us by a commodius vicus of recirculation back"; presented next are the chaotic materials of the entire book in a paragraph of proto-history; then follows a summary of human history: the fall—metaphorically represented by Finnegan of the Irish ballad—the two kinds of activity, love and war, which make up the entire spectrum of life, so far as Joyce is concerned, the sense of guilt with which man is eternally burdened—like a hump on his back—and the cycles of death and birth which continually contribute relics, memories and museum pieces to the human scene. Ireland and the area surrounding Dublin are introduced as representative of the world. The records of four periods of history are referred to as incomplete; somewhere, in the "silent" gap between 566 "antediluvious" and 566 "annadominant," a scroll has been lost. Prehistoric types, Mutt and Jute, gaze on the upturned evidences of the old civilization whose history is presumably recorded in the lost and rediscovered "claybook." There follows a discussion of the development of language, culminating in a statement about a complicated "book of Doublends Jined (may his forehead be darkened with mud who would sunder!) till Daleth, mahomahouma, who oped it closeth thereof the. Dor" (20.15–18. "Daleth" = "door" in Hebrew). The associative implications of the marriage ceremony—"whomever God hath joined together, let no man put asunder"; "till death us do part"—suggest the end of one state of being and, by the opening of a door, the initiation into another, which, in turn, will end with the closing of the door. Then comes an admonition to wait before giving way to tears, because there are lots of stories to be told before that door is closed, all to do with temptresses and wives, sins of men and boys.[5] This paragraph ends with the sound of urination, the "rain" that announces the entrance of the Prankquean and the beginning of the first three-part myth of *Finnegans Wake*, Joyce's version of the "fortunate fall."

The "three-times-is-a-charm" motif runs like a musical theme-with-variations throughout the book. It is associated with the structural system of cycles: the Viconian rhythm of three ages and *ricorso*, the units of three tones and an interval, three attacks and a pause, three surges and a change, and the fairytale pattern of three tries and a magic "opening." The episodes in *Finnegans Wake* always demonstrate the implicit allegation of the author that war and love, the two basic functions of mankind, inevitably follow one another—indeed, are inextricably conjoined.

The Prankquean story begins in a stone age—"an auldstane eld, when Adam was delvin and his madameen spinning watersilts" (21.5–6), and its protagonists are "hill" and "rill" (23.17). But the entire Earwicker family of five is foreshadowed in the story. HCE as the Earl of Howth assumes names and aspects which connect him with giant, mountain, wind, porter (door-keeper), and old man; ALP acts the part of Grace O'Malley, has the attributes of "niece"-temptress, mother, rain, river, her "madesty," the Pee Queen and the "prank wench" Pranky Ann (Pranque / An), at once a representation of the wife and the daughter who acts as a leap-year temptress in a later riddle story; the gloomy Shem plays the tree, as well as the part of Tristopher, the converted "luderman" (playboy and Luther-man); and sunny Shaun—Hilary, changed to the sad "Tristian"—is the hill who anticipates the mountain aspect of his father; the dummy, with whom Hilary plays "like brodar and histher" and whom Toughertrees (the converted Tristopher) mauls and kisses "like knavepaltry and naivebride and in their second infancy," is the proto-type of Issy, naughty daughter of HCE and ALP.

The tale is based on the Irish legend of the visit of Grace O'Malley to the castle of the Earl of Howth, for which Adaline Glasheen's entry in *A Second Census* may serve as a short summary.

> According to report, she sailed up to Howth, went to the Castle and demanded admission. The Earl of Howth refused her because he was at dinner. In revenge, she kid-napped his young heir and did not return him until the Earl promised that his doors would always stand open at mealtime.[6]

For an analytical reading, I have rearranged the elements of the story so that each visit of the Prankquean can be compared with the other two.

On the first encounter, Jarl van Hoother is described as a dead match ("burnt head") or an unlit wick of a

Visits	#1	#2	#3
Conditions	dry	rain	storm
Jarl	his burnt head high up in his lamphouse laying cold hands on himself	his baretholobruised heels drowned [down] in his cellarmalt shaking warm hands with himself	his hurricane hips up to his pantry box ruminating in his holdfour stomachs
Jiminies and Dummy	Tristopher and Hilary cousins of ourn	Hilary and dummy in first infancy	Toughertrees and dummy like knavepaltry and naive-bride in second infancy
	kickaheeling their dummy	wringing and coughing like brodar and histher below on the tearsheet	kissing and spitting, and roguing and poghuing belove on the watercloth
	on oil cloth flure of homerigh, castle and earthenhouse*		
	be dermot	be redtom†	be dom ter†
Prankquean	the niece-of-his-in-law come to the keep of his inn	come . . . to the bar of his bristolry	halt . . . by the ward of his mansionhome
	pulled a rosy one made her wit foreninst the dour	nipped a paly one made her witter before the wicked	picked a blank made her wittest in front of the arkway of trihump
	lit up fireland was ablaze	lit up redcocks flew flackering from the hillcombs	lit out valleys lay twinkling

6

	spoke to the dour in her petty perusienne	saying	asking
Riddle	Mark the Wans why do I am alook alike a poss of porterpease? how the skirtmisshes began	Mark the Twy why do I am alook alike two poss of porterpease?	Mark the Tris why do I am alook alike three poss of porter pease? how the skirtmishes endupped
Answer	The dour handworded [antwortet=answered (Germ.)] her grace in dootch nossow Shut	says the wicked, handwording her madesty Shut	Jarl van Hoother Boanerges terror of the dames came hip hop handihap out through the pikeopened arkway of his three shuttoned castles he ordurd shut up shop, dappy
Result	grace o'malice kidsnapped Tristopher into shandy westerness she rain, rain, rain	her madesty set down a jiminy and took up a jiminy all the lilipath ways to Woeman's land she rain, rain, rain	the duppy shot the shutter clup [Thunder] And they all drank free
van Hoother	warlessed after her with soft dovesgall Stop deef stop come back to my earin stop	bleethered atter her with loud finegale Stop domb stop Come back with my earring stop	
The Prankquean	swaradid	swaradid	

7

Visits	#1 Unlikelihud	#2 Am liking it	#3
	a brannewail [brand new cry of fire] that same sabboath night of falling angles somewhere in Erio	a wild old grannewwail [Granu Wail=Grace O'Malley (Irish)] that laurency night of starshootings somewhere in Erio	
The Prankquean	went for her forty years' walk in Tourlemonde washed blessings of love spots off the jiminy with soap sulliver suddles	went for her forty years' walk in Turnlemeem punched curses of cromcruwell with the nail of a top into the jiminy	
	her four owlers masters tauch him his tickles convorted him to the onesure allgood he became a luderman	the four larksical monitrix touch him his tears provorted him to the onecertain allsecure he became a tristian	
	she started to rain and to rain	she started raining, raining	
	back again in a brace of samers the jiminy in her pinafrond lace at night another time	back again in a pair of changers Larryhill under her abromette another nice lace for the third charm	

* van Hoother, HCE, and Vanhomrigh (father of Swift's Vanessa) are related by this phrase.
† These are variations of "Dermot" with whom Grania ran away rather than marry old Finn MacCool.

lamp. Conditions are dry; the jiminies play on an oilcloth
"flure" and the combustibility suggested by oil is confirmed
by the fact that the fire (desire) brought to the sour, cold,
masturbating Jarl sets all Ireland ("fireland") ablaze. But
the Prankquean also wets against his door—actually, *he* is
the door ("dour") as well as the porter, the doorkeeper—
bringing him water in addition to fire, and she asks him the
riddle, the answer to which not only explains his dead
condition but is also the key to his revivification. In translation, it goes something like this: "Mark I, why am I and
a poss of porter as much alike as peas (in a pod)?"[7] The
obvious answer is that, like the porter (ale), she, too, is
firewater, and is the cause of man's fall. This is only a basic
interpretation of the riddle, of course. The Prankquean's
urine is like the porter, and as symbol of the renewing
firewater—whisky for Tim Finnegan—is a sustained motif
throughout *Finnegans Wake*. "Porter" is a loaded word in
the book, referring always to doorkeeping as well as to
ale and to other things; it will be remembered that the
Earwicker family, in the bedroom chapter (III, iv), has
the name of Porter. At any rate, the first encounter only
dampens the dour, which (or who), as he answers her
grace in German, shuts (*double entendre*) in her face. The
dour is also defiantly challenging her to do her worst, for
"schütten," in German, means to "pour." The Pee Queen,
who has brought majesty to the Jarl's door, takes her
"reign" and the kidnapped Tristopher west, where her
fertility is wasted on barren soil. "And that was how the
skirtmisshes began." "Mische-mische," partially heard in
the word "skirtmisshes," is the woman's "I am" affirmation;
it is usually found in conjunction with the phrase "tauf-
tauf" (taufen = baptism [German]) or a distortion of it,
and consistently connotes urination. Although the Jarl calls
after her not to be deaf but to come back to Erin, within
hearing, her answer is "unlikelihud." And she leaves behind

a cry of fire (brannewail: Danish "brand" = fire) and the wail of falling angels, a description which calls to mind the war in Heaven as preliminary to man's fall.

The second encounter is wetter and warmer. Jarl von Hoother has been drowning his sorrows (but heightening his desire) in the cellarmalt, and "shaking warm hands with himself." Hilary and the dummy play on a sheet of tears (the dummy is here associated with Doll Tearsheet), and there are other indications of rain. The Prankquean produces something like lightning this time, doubles the amount of "porter" in her riddle, and makes the "wicked" (wicket), Mark II, even "witter" than before. The wicket gate is shut against "her madesty" ("modesty," or genitals) and, with another jiminy, she sets out for Woeman's (noman's; woman's) land with her royal rain. Now the earl is beginning to contribute to the storm. He blows after her "with a loud finegale,"[8] and, when she returns for the third time, his "hurricane hips" are "up to his pantry-box," and the rumble of approaching thunder is beginning in his "holdfour stomachs." Toughertrees and the dummy are play-acting "on the watercloth" a miniature of the larger drama that is about to take place. The Prankquean's siege includes a direct attack on the door this time: she "picked a blank" and her lighting-up sprinkles the valley with stars. The door is now an "arkway of trihump" (which phrase contains a reference to humpbacked HCE with his phallic triple weapon, as well as to the well-known Arc de Triomphe), and is open and ready for the emergence of the "old terror of the dames" himself, a "match" any day, when he is drenched in firewater, for a tricky temptress.

As usual, when Joyce comes to the sexual climax of whatever tale he is telling, he increases the linguistic anthropomorphizing of parts of the body, muddles the narrative by heightened metaphor and, through obscure combinations, provides for multiple interpretations of the action. The Jarl is made to act, but what does he do? Well, it is clear that his orduring with thunder is defecation, and, in *Finnegans Wake*, defecation always stands for creation; but one can't ignore the fact that the opening is for the "trihump"—the "three shuttoned castles"—that "he" comes out "to the whole longth of the strongth of his bowman's bill," and that "one man in his armour" being a "fat match always for any girls under shurts" undoubtedly refers to the male member in erection. The action is dual, then; it includes the build-up, the erection, the creative power of both intercourse and defecation, and the fall. "And that was the first peace [settlement of the siege; piece] of illiterative porthery [poetry; but includes porter, porte, pother, Arthur, and perhaps "porthole," as "a loophole in the wall of a fort for shooting through" (dictionary) and as a connection with the sea story of the Norwegian Captain] in all the flamend floody [fire; water] flatuous [windy] world" (23.9–10). Yawn, commenting on the same dualistic action (in III, iii) says:

> —He could claud boose his eyes to the birth of his garce, he could lump all his lot through the half of her play, but he jest couldn't laugh through the whole of her farce becorpse he warn't billed that way. So he outandouts his volimetangere [a highlycharged "noli-me-tangere" (touch-me-not) converted into voli-me-tangere—*do* touch me (Latin *voli* = "do")] and has a lightning consultation and he downadowns his pantoloogions and made a piece of first perpersonal puetry that staystale remains to be. Cleaned. (509.30–36)

I presume that the heirs are snatched in a doubled-up deference to the original Grace O'Malley legend, but the kidnappings also link the action to the legend of Dermot and Grania.[9] Each time the Prankquean kidnaps a jiminy, she is running off with a younger man, as Grania did with Dermot, but she finally marries the older man, as Grania married Finn MacCool. The jiminies' names, Hilary and Tristopher, which were, no doubt, taken from Bruno's motto, *"Hilaris in tristitia, tristis in hilaritate,"* are appropriate to the paradoxical theme of the fortunate fall. The dummy does not act, except to shut the last door, and she immediately becomes the property of the Prankquean.[10]

Obviously, all of this partially-concealed erotic imagery in a parodic account of the fall of our first parents contributes to the scatological humor of the book. It is psychologically consistent as well, however, with Freudian dream-theory and the primal significance attributed to the sexual drive. Moreover, Joyce is as Irish-Catholic as he can be when he interprets the original sin to be sexual. But his "theology" becomes exceedingly Miltonic in the repeated emphasis upon sex as an important creative act, the beginning of man as man. Promethean defiance, too, is evident in the story; such "sin" is, in effect, man's historical salvation. And the "crime" of creative art is consistently exalted in the images of defecation. That thunder announces the creation of the word.

After the thunderword and the simultaneous shutting of the door, images of the immediate narrative are merged with preview pictures of the Norwegian Captain tale, not to be told until II, iii. "The prankquean was to hold her dummyship and the jiminies was to keep the peacewave and van Hoother was to git the wind up" (23.12–14). The picture is one of a cooperative effort to keep a ship at sea afloat. After all, we ought to expect some reference to a flood, following all the raining of the Prankquean.[11] Moreover, Joyce summarizes the Prankquean story by the comment: "How kirssy the tiler made a sweet unclose to the Narwhealian captol. Saw fore shalt thou sea" (23.10–12). A reference to the visits and sailings of the Norwegian captain seems, at first, to be out of place. But the language provides a connection, which, it will be seen, is justified on grounds both thematic and structurally esthetic. "Sweet unclose" means not only "suit of clothes" but also "sweet opening"—or the unclosing of a door. And the Narwhal is a male cetacean with a long, straight, spiral tusk—not unlike the Jarl's "bowman's bill," presumably. Still, if the Prankquean is responsible for the opening of the door in the immediate story, what has she to do with Kersse the tailor? Finnegan's "missus," the "queenoveire" (of Eire; of Fire) is referred to as "the tailor's daughter" by one of the four old men—she who is "waiting for winter to fire the enchantement, decoying more nesters to fall down the flue" (28.8–9). And the admiring oldster remembers how Finnegan handled her "so she never knew was she on land or at sea or swooped through the blue like Airwinger's bride" (28.14–15). The correspondence between the two stories is definitely established in this first chapter and will warrant further investigation.

I think there is no doubt that the outcome of the Prankquean story is a royal "marriage." The call, for which there is "Noanswa" (23.20–21), to the preoccupied ones behind the door is to "Homfrie" and "Livia," king and queen (like Victoria and Albert, for whom the lakes *Victoria Nyanza* and *Albert*, at the source of the Nile, were named). Moreover, a passage on 508.6 recalls the Prankquean story as a "Pax and Quantum wedding" (wetting). Of course Issy, in later scenes, is an incarnation of her mother, just as ALP is a naughty precursor of herself. The bewildering role-switching of Humphrey's and Anna's twins is also foreshadowed in this early story, when the sad twin is tickled into laughter and the hilarious twin is taught his tears. The replacement of the old man by the new may be suggested by the progressive titles, "Mark the Wans," "Mark the Twy," and "Mark the Tris," but I believe that the amalgamation of the sons with the father is more important. The name, "Jarl von Hoother Boanerges," includes the "orduring" earl and the two sons of thunder, James and John. The "three-times-is-a-charm" motif and the temptation theme are firmly established; they will be modified in the three attempts of Glugg to solve the heliotrope riddle, and so to guess correctly in the Colours Game; they will be reversed in the Norwegian Captain story and perverted in the account of how Buckley shot the Russian general—and the rhythms of the Prankquean legend will permeate the entire book. The Prankquean story, then, though not strictly a generating episode, can be regarded as the prime example of a tripartite pattern which is not only repeated again and again but which, with the addition of the Viconian *ricorso*, comprises the total structure of the *Wake*.

One thing is certain: Whatever happened behind the door is a source of both guilt and grace. The exclamation, "O foenix culprit" *(felix culpa)*, recalls Adam's fortunate fall through woman and gives a hint as to what, besides the HCE-Hill of Howth connection, caused Joyce to use as basis for his tale the old legend of Grace O'Malley, for the name of this female pirate, metamorphosed into "grace o'malice" (21.20–21), also means good out of evil. Joyce repeats the theme in Djoytsch Latin: "Ex nickylow malo comes mickelmassed bonum" (23.16–17). What goes on between man and woman behind closed doors is, or should be, a secret; neither partner will answer. But the hill is caught by the water—"landloughed by his neaghboormistress" (23.29) —and is both perpetuated in and petrified by his children—"perpetrified in his offsprung" (23.39–30). Poets could tell them both to their faces that, except for them, there wouldn't be a spire in the town nor any "yew nor an eye" at all. The episode and its commentary close with the word "*Usqueadbaugham,*" enclosing the name Adam in the Irish word for whisky, the firewater associated with woman which is responsible for Finnegan's fall and for his awakening, and for all similar erections, creations, falls, and subsequent baptismal reanimation.[12]

Although, in a few places, the Jarl seems to be one of the twins, the bulk of the evidence assigns this role to HCE and his Finnegan-Finn MacCool-Mark of Cornwall-predecessors. A part of HCE's self-justification (532.16–18) alleges "I am as cleanliving as could be and . . . my game was a fair average since I perpetually kept my ouija ouija wicket up." The word "wicket" reaches back to the Prankquean episode, and the stuttering ("ouija, ouija") indicates that Earwicker is experiencing guilt about this ambiguous statement; he did *not* keep his wicket gate shut up, but he did get his "wicked" up. In a summary of his sins and coming old age, after his last attempt at intercourse with Anna, the language again connects HCE to the gate event (Finneganese for "great door event"): "That's his last tryon to march through the grand tryomphal arch. His reignbolt's shot. Never again!" (590.9–10) . This sentence links the consummation event of the Prankquean story to the final sexual incident in Humphrey's and Anna's marriage; proves that marching through the door means intercourse; and confirms the idea that the Prankquean's wetting was, in repetitious effect, the *reine* bringing the reign to the Jarl, thereby giving him the royal rein. But after this late attempt he is about to lose his kingly title. At dawn, he finds it hard to get out of bed. "So let him slap [sleep], the sap! Till they take down his shatter from his shap. He canease" (595.31–32) . The last phrase, meaning "he can take his ease," corresponds with the Prankquean's "petty perusienne" and the Jarl's "dootch"; HCE is referred to in HEC-anese, his own brand of speech.

I have been able to find only one indication that the Jarl and Shem are dubiously identified by Prankquean diction encompassed in the description of Shem's abode (I, vii) , the "house O'Shea or O'Shame, *Quivapieno*, known as the Haunted Inkbottle, no number Brimstone Walk, Asia in Ireland, as it was infested with the raps, with his penname SHUT sepiacraped on the doorplate and a blind of black sailcloth over its wan phwinshogue" (182.30–33). There are numerous references to firewater—and Shem's aversion to it[13]—in his chapter, but he seems to be notoriously "showerproof" (182.16). It will be seen in the "Mime" episode (II, i) that, alone, he is doomed to ineffectual action after his triple chance at the heliotrope riddle in the game of Colours. And Shaun's independent claims to Jarl-ship can be easily discounted as the uneasy assertions of a pretender. In his admonishments to his sister, he worries about someone who might tempt her to "open the door softly" and call her "bump, like a blizz, in the muezzin of the turkest night" (442.32–33). He blusters, protectively, that he might turn the fellow over to the police; "Or for that matter, for your information, if I get the wind up what do you bet in the buckets of my wrath I mightn't even take it into my progromme, as sweet course, to do a rash act" (443.6–7). And, after many more warnings, he says, "If I've proved to your sallysfashion how I'm a man of Armor let me so, let me sue, let me see your isabellis (446.5–7).[14] Shaun, here, is not only trying to assume the father role but is attempting to persuade his sister of his Hilary-to-Tristram (Tristopher) transformation.

If one needs proof that the Prankquean is ALP in disguise (Anna = "Grace," in Hebrew), the firmest connections can be found in the sections dealing specifically with the rivermother. "So tellus tellas allabouter. The why or whether she looked alottylike like ussies and whether he had his wimdop like themses shut?" (101.2–4). If the reader's ear is well tuned, he will immediately detect overtones of the "Why am I alook alike" rhythm, and will recognize the "git the wind up" sounds in "wimdop," which also means a window—"up" or shut.[15] Again, the same section refers to ALP as she who *shut*tered him after his fall and waked him widowt sparing and gave him keen and made him able ... stood forth, burn*zburn* the gorggony old danworld ... finickin here and funickin there, with her louise*quean*'s brogues ... riding her *Parisienne*'s cockneze ... with *p*awns, *p*relates and *p*ookas *p*elotting in her *p*iecebag, for Handiman the Chomp, Esquoro.   (102.1–16)

I have italicized the elements which relate this citation, by language, to the Prankquean. It should be evident that wherever an inordinate aggregation of p's occurs, the Pee Queen is alluded to. (It is also apparent that a distinct meaning is given to "shut" here, having to do with wifely protectiveness and possessiveness after the fall.) Another unmistakable identification occurs in the answer to the second question of Shem's quiz (I, vi), the one applying to the "mutter," Anna Livia: "If *hot* Hammurabi, or *cowld* Clesiastes, could espy her *prank*lings, they'd burst bounds agin" (139.25–27; italics mine). The most lengthy reminder of the Prankquean events as pertaining to HCE and ALP, however, is to be found in the last chapter, where the old wife takes her aging husband for a walk and suggests a visit to the "Old Lord." (Again, I have italicized the pertinent words and bracketed some interpretations.)

His *door* always open. For a newera's day. Much as your own is. You invoiced him last Eatster so he ought to give us hockockles and everything. Remember to take off your white hat, ech? When we come in the presence. And say hoothoothoo, ithmuthisthy [how do you do (*Hoother* two, too) his (your) majesty]! His is house of laws. And I'll drop my *graci*ast *kertssey* too.[16] If the Ming Tung no go bo to me homage me hamage kow bow tow to the Mong Tang [If the mountain won't go bow to Mohammed, etc.]. Ceremonialness to stand lowest place be! Saying: *What'll you take to link to light a pike* [girl (Norwegian)] *on porpoise, plaise?* He might knight you an *Armor* elsor daub you the first cheap *magyerstrape.*[17] Remember *Bomtho-*

manew ["baretholobruised"; Bartholomew] vim vam vom Hungerig. Hoteform, chain and epolettes [HCE in regal uniform—plus chain] botherbumbose [his paradoxical position]. And I'll be your aural eyeness [royal highness]. (623.6–18)

Anna Livia goes on to say that this talk is just "plain fancies"; those old days are past. She has already admitted that, although her "herewaker of our hamefame" will "get himself up and erect, confident and heroic," it will not be for her any more but when, "young as of old, for my daily comfreshenall, a wee one woos" (619.12–15). So, if everything recurs, the "sehm asnuh," the daughter *will be* the Prankquean and *was* the Prankquean in a youthful version of ALP. The Jarl, however, is an older man; that is why he is called "Mark," in the riddle, and the Prankquean is called, in a deliberately confusing manner, "the niece-of-his-in-law." The story, then, ties in with another major motif of *Finnegans Wake,* the mutual seduction between an older man and a very young girl, which makes use of numerous historical and legendary relationships—e.g., Swift and the "Stellas," Mark and Isolde, Lewis Carroll and Alice, Finn MacCool and Grania. In another context, dealing with an encounter between a young girl and a priestly pervert, the Grace O'Malley legend is again recalled: "whyre have you been so grace a mauling and where were you chaste me child?" (115.19–20) .

It seems to me that the Prankquean story, by the time its echoes are traced and categorized, illustrates in a manner fairly easy to comprehend Joyce's treatment of composite woman and composite man. One can use the term "replacement" to apply to both processes of changing relationships, but the development for each is slightly different. The interplay of the female "two" and the male "three" will be discussed at length in another chapter, but, in connection with the Prankquean story, we can note that the two female elements, the Prankquean and the dummy, present three possibilities: They might be viewed as *1*] ALP and an adopted daughter, *2*] Issy and her imaginary companion—in this case referred to as a dummy or doll— or *3*] the composite daughter-wife as exemplified by the Prankquean plus a lifeless prototype of the "wee one" to come. The story is odd as a version of the creative fall in that the two sons are already in existence with the Jarl when the Prankquean brings the life-giving firewater to the castle. Since the dummy seems to be lifeless—at least passive, except for the shutting of the door—I think we can discard possibility number one. One particular passage referring to the Porters' daughter makes number two tempting: "Pussy is never alone, as records her chambrette, for she can always look at Biddles and talk petnames with her little playfilly when she is sitting downy on the ploshmat" ("floor," in an early draft). "Ah Biddles es ma plikplak," she coos. "Ah plikplak wed ma Biddles" (561.35–562.3). But the dummy on the "flure" in the Prankquean story does not talk, even to itself, and seems to be merely a toy for the twins. It can hardly be the Prankquean's imaginary companion or even her mirror reflection. On the other hand, P and Q are referred to as "sisters" by the interrogating old man in III, iii:

> —Concaving now convexly to the semidemihemispheres and, from the female angle, music minnestirring, were the subligate sisters, P. and Q., Clopatrick's cherierapest, *mutatis mutandis*, in pretty much the same pickle, the peach of all piedom, the quest of all quicks?
> —Peequeen ourselves, the prettiest pickles of unmatchemable mute antes I ever bopeeped at, seesaw shallshee, since the town go went gonning on Pranksome Quaine. (508.21–28)

The unmistakable connection is between the Prankquean and the two girls in the park—and while this is important for our discussion of the "two," it does not seem logical to count the dummy as a second temptress of the Jarl. More than likely, the dummy represents the as-yet-unborn replacement for the dualistic daughter-wife, the "Peena and Queena . . . duetting a giggle-for-giggle" (377.18–19). The acceptance of this last possibility will become easier after we examine the Prankquean and the Norwegian Captain's story together.[18]

On the inside of the castle is a male trio. Since the "marriage" has not yet occurred, we must assume that the three are composite parts of the whole man. There is no "dummy" for the male offspring who are to come. These two, Tristopher and Hilary, are opposite elements of the "old man," who is to fall, become converted (the "conversion" of the twins is an indication), be thrice baptized, and be born again into vigorously fertile life as he crosses the threshold of the all-important door. Using a metaphor that becomes of major importance in the book, we can say that the Jarl is the two-branched tea tree with dead leaves that must be wet by woman to become rejuvenated, just as he is the dead match that must be lit by her fire. This whole story, therefore, becomes extremely significant as the first sustained illustration of how Joyce will continually employ an inverted synecdoche—the whole representing the parts, the multiple standing for the one—to advance his homely theme of recurrent life. It will take only a cursory analysis of three episodes related to the Prankquean story to show how complicated this homely theme can get.

2] *The Game of Colours*

THE "Mime" chapter (II, i) presents the three Ear-wicker children mimicking their elders in a play version of the seduction story. Although the game of "Angels and Devils or colours"[19] is a metaphor for the positions of all children in relation to all parents, the most striking first impression of the action is not its symbolism but its re-semblance to conventional naturalistic dramatization and its revelation of the personalities of the three youngsters, Shem, Shaun, and Issy, as their own imaginations and idiosyncracies heighten the experience of the game. A sum-mary of what happens on the naturalistic level will do the double service of defining these character traits and explain-ing the symbolic significance of the drama.

The action is presented as a stage performance, for which a cast of characters is listed and other credits are given, before the play begins. "Mr Seumas McQuillad" (Shem the Penman) plays Glugg, the bad boy or devil; "Miss Butys Pott" (Issy) is the leading lady, Izod, and she has her girl scout friends in to form her flower "guard"; "Mr Sean O'Mailey" (Shaun the Post) is the good boy, or angel, Chuff. Short appearances are made by the woman and the man of the house, Ann and Hump. The customers of the pub provide background noise and the two servants, although they do not speak, apparently have walk-on parts, since they are listed with the cast. Mentioned with the list of credits are many recognizable properties which lead us to expect that the drama will have a familiar, recurrent theme: blood and thunder, the four horsemen of the Apocalypse, Finnegan, the Flood, a pipe and a hat, a tree and a rock, doorposts, lightning and fire, the mountain and the river—all making up a Pageant of Past History. And the argument is as follows:[20]

Chuff is a protecting angel (222.22), whose sword flashes as he makes the sign of the cross. Glugg, the devilish one, is lost to learning, gnashing his teeth over books and devoting himself to low pursuits ("makes prayses to his three of clubs": one of the many references to Glugg's masturbation in the mime account). The girls are twittering and beckoning behind Glugg's back. Mirrylamb (Izod) is nervous (223.1–2). She worries that, in spite of all her signals, Glugg will not guess her color and catch her for his bride. She acts out a charade for his clue. "I am (twintomine) all thees thing. Up tighty in the front, down again on the loose, drim and drumming on her back and a pop from her whistle. What is that, O holytroopers? Isot givin yoe?" All of which Shem should have interpreted as: "Up to T [the "he" symbol] in the front, down again on the 'lio's,' 'tr'im and drumming on her back and a pop ["p" sound] from her whistle. The answer is 'heliotrope.' Is it given you? Give in?" Or, in terms of Izod's real desire, as a description of the sexual act: "Up with the T in the front, down again when it's 'loose'—she on her back and peeing from her whistle. Is a 'T' given you? Are you virile? Shall Izod be given to you?"[21] (Cf. the discussion, above, of the Pee Queen. Sex, with Joyce, is always "mixturated.") He comes to her, his first "quest." But Glugg is fated for a fall. "Stop," says "the evangelion," Chuff; and Glugg stops. He offers the girl a "trifle from the grass." Perhaps his T-rifle is only a trifle and he has spilled his "tea" on the grass.

It is not clear who asks the questions, "Who are you?" and "What do you lack?" and who gives the answers. Perhaps it is Glugg seeking clues and getting nowhere, or perhaps it is Chuff exercising a ritual of the game, getting wrong answers from Glugg. Anyway, Glugg racks his brains to figure out what it is he is going to "prehend." How to word it is what he must discover. And a dark, perilous time is coming when he will be able to guess no longer—nor see the colors. Three anagrams of the word he seeks are given in the text: "O theoperil! Ethiaop lore, the poor lie." He asks for an answer from the four gospels, from the four elements (the last one being water, to which he listens "how she pranked alone so johntily"), and from the "wordless" ass. He becomes "hardset," but, instead of sex, all he thinks about is that he has to "go (somewhere) while he was weeting." He wishes a grave for the four to grieve them. His "hardset" becomes rubbery ("goodda purssia" = gutta percha) and then pure "injine ruber" (224.2–3). He would like to give the four a present of this limp corpse. And this is what he wishes: that he found the four and fouled the ford; that he threw stones at them and they fell into the grave he dug; that he then sat down with the rest of the feast (roast meat).[22]

Whereby hangs our tale and Glugg's tail.

But Glugg's Oedipus complex is to blame: his "towerable" fear of his "colline born" father—whom the boy remembers as all lit up when his "fontmouther" tempted him with her "How do you do that lack a lock and pass the poker, please?" and his "deplurabel" tie to his sick mother. In his subconscious mind is buried the answer to whether or not he has murdered his mother, or whether he merely misses her. "Misty's trompe or midst his flooting?" Perhaps he is impotent because of her.

Now the girls have lined up behind Chuff, and Glugg must guess their colors, asking his questions of "their commoner guardian" (who is really the "rapier" of the two, although Glugg can "hold his own . . . with his hand") . Glugg decides to be funny and use his "art" in a preliminary jesting question with *double entendre*: "Have you, perhaps, carbunckly ones?" The girls laugh (225.1) , pretend to be offended, say for him to go tell it to the marines, hold their noses and insinuate that he "make[s] peace in his preaches and play[s] with esteem."

Chuff yells "Toboo!" and Glugg runs off, squatting down and suffering—or pretending to suffer—from a stomach ache. Izod comes to him—her first advance to get him to speak. (He has gone to face her once; she now comes to him.) She didn't mean anything. But he's so dumb. If he'd only talk instead of gawk and worry so. "Speak, sweety bird![23] Mitzymitzy [mische mische]! Though I did ate tough turf [tauf tauf] I'm not the bogdoxy." So he makes his three guesses, and experiences his first failure, for his "colors" are associated with brimstone, hell fire, and demon's land, not with sun and heaven.

The girls dance around Chuff in his heaven; but Izod cries (226.4) , sits glooming. "Her beauman's gone of a cool." She will not be the sun-girl much longer. "She is fading out" like the close of day, and will have to meet "anew fiancy" among the shades. For a dame has a damsel and a damsel has a dolly, but damsel turns to dame and dame grows old with the passing of time.[24] The girls dance in a routine that illustrates the growing-old process and then the fresh renewal of life. They are counted first of all in normal succession, spelling the word "RAYNBOW"; then they represent (227.3–14) their future older selves as the colors are reversed: Winnie, Olive and Beatrice, Nelly and Ida, Amy and Rue.

Meanwhile, Glugg is in a rage, because "he don't know whose hue." He swears, fumes, threatens to go to sea (228.7–9) , to run away and, by employing silence, exile and cunning, to write a foul book, to be finished in "ge-trennty years," his "farced epistol to the hibruws." He will go in for Small Profits and Quick Returns (229.7) and will tell the public all about that tea lady and her knave ("the lalage of lyonesses,[25] and him, her knave arrant.") Distortions of the titles for the *Ulysses* chapters follow. Glugg will gossip about his parents and call it confession. Then he will show that dame (230.11–24). He'll become a poet and write sentimental poetry about his loss of home, and make them all feel sorry (231.1–8). To top it all, he gets a toothache "Like gnawthing unheardth"; however, he has passed imaginatively through exorcism. He throws a fit, but the worst is over (232.5). Then he gets a message from Izod, her second advance to him: "cumbeck to errind." Stop crying. Sit in my lap.

So he dashes back—like father, like son—over the sea (figuratively) for the second set of three guesses. This time he makes no puns but is in earnest (233.19–20). The answers, however, are "Nao" (that's the way non-exiles pronounce "know"), and he slinks away in foul spirits (234.1–2); again, his "spear" it's all fallen on him ("his sperrits all foulen on him"). He looks like bloody hell, this "cock-shy" Don Quixote, whereas his Sancho Panza brother remains behind, a winsome churl. The little "dulsy nayers" surround the latter, ask him to get the "argan" bellowsed up so that they can sing hymns, and they profanely worship (235.9–236.18), with many prophecies about the future heavenly mansion of Izod-Isolde and Tristram-Chuff, the sunny, god-like son. This love ritual, including the dances of the flowers and the eating of the god (236.19–32), has been repeated for ages, as the distortion of the Quinet passage[26] reminds us; even when Pa's "horns" are dumb, his T-cups obsolete and empty, when he has become obese and ma mummified, the dancing hours are as lithe and limber as before: "those danceadeils and cancanzanies have come

stimmering down for our begayment through the bedeaf-
dom of po's taeorns, the obcecity of pa's teapucs, as lithe
and limbfree limber as when momie mummed at ma."

The girls praise Chuff, but their admiration is for
his purity: "your intercourse at ninety legsplits does not
defile." They want, posthaste, tickets (tickles) before the
"letter" arrives (238.2). In fact, they are all for independ-
ence and free love (239.12–14). Behold our handmaids for
the Lord. Right now, we are yours, but we hope for the
day when we shall be ours. No more giving in marriage. To
each her own fancy. Hightime!

> When every Klitty of a scolderymeid shall hold every
> yardscullion's right to stimm her uprecht for whimsoever,
> whether on privates, whather in publics. And when all us
> romance catholeens shall have ones for all amanseprated.
> And the world is maidfree. Methanks. So much for His
> Meignysthy man! And all his bigyttens.   (239.18–23)

The girls thank God for man, but as for the presence of
that Most High, "where the diggings he dwellst amongst
us here's nobody knows save Mary."

As these "bright elects" waltz, "oaths and screams
and bawley groans" can be heard as if issuing from Hell.
Glugg lies foul end up in his grave. But he rises and makes
a mock repentance (240.5–7), in order to earn a third
chance. No more, he says, will he be forever sitting on the
"stool," regarding his own tumescence (he means, as well as
toilet seat, the "domstol," [Danish] seat of judgment; so
he promises to give up constant judging, criticizing). His
"dome" has been muddied by trinities (preoccupied with
the "three of clubs"); now he will play for eternities (be
holy, like Shaun). He apologizes for all his father's sins,
and then discusses his father's helpmeet and their marriage
bargain (241.1–243.36).

The moon comes up (244.3–4). The Feast of Tabernacles is near.[27] Darkness and obscurity will soon usurp the place of the sun-god. The home of the father and mother is described as an ark, to which all the creatures of the world must retire and be viewed in microcosmic isolation. The thunder, announcing the rain and the end of this particular phase of the human drama, will presently be heard. There is a pause in the stage war (246.3–6), as "Housefather calls enthreateningly." But before they leave the game, Glugg must have his third chance, for "ein and twee were never worth three. So they must have their final since he's on parole," in order for Izod to choose between the two rivals. "For she must walk out. And it must be with who. Teaseforhim. Toesforhim. Tossforhim. Two. Else there is danger of. Solitude."

They are ready again for the fray. "Postreintroducing Jeremy," or Glugg. He knows he hasn't much of a chance. He weeps. He seemed to love his sweetheart as a boy. Mourning for his mom, he sees the future. He doesn't want to give up love in favor of his twin. Immaculacy (celibacy) must change its clothes; he must change his tune. So he wars with himself. He wants the girl; he will try. He goes to her. She offers him another charade on the word "heliotrope": "Clap your lingua to your pallet ["he"], drop your jowl with a jolt ["lio"], tambourine until your breath slides ["tro"], pet a pout ["pe"] and it's out. Have you got me, Allysloper?" Then she gives him so many riddling hints that his head is reeling. (There are at least twelve conundrums on the word "heliotrope." I offer a few interpretations.) "My top it was brought Achill's low ["heel"], my middle I ope ["io"] before you, my bottom's a vulser if ever there valsed ["trope" (waltz "turn")] and my whole the flower that stars the day and is solly well worth your pilger's fahrt ["heliotrope," the "sol"-flower]." As she continues her hints, the syllables of the word get all mixed up. "Where there's a hitch ["h"], a head of things, let henker's halter ["rope"] hang the halunkenend. For I see through your weapon ["T"]. That cry's not Cucullus [but "hel (p) "]. And his eyelids ["i"] are painted. If my tutor here is cut out for an oldeborre ["o"] I'm Flo, shy of peeps ["p's"], you know." She refers to the "holy 'T' rape" of the river by Michael Arklow, the priest of Glendalough ("Luggelaw." Cf. 203.16–26 and 604–606). She tries allusions to the kinds of erudite material this "lost-to-learning" ought to recognize. "Awabeg [Arabic H] is my callby, Magnus [El] here's my Max, Wonder One's [I] my cipher [O] and Seven Sisters [the "troop"] is my nighbrood." She describes the sensual qualities of the word's sounds, its rising and falling structural pattern, and its total possible voluptuous meaning for the two who understand it together:

> In the house of breathings lies that word, all fairness. The walls are of rubinen and the glittergates of elfinbone. The roof herof is of massicious jasper and a canopy of Tyrian awning rises and still descends to it. A grape cluster of lights hangs therebeneath and all the house is filled with the breathings of her fairness, the fairness of fondance and the fairness of milk and rhubarb and the fairness of roasted meats and uniomargrits and the fairness of promise with consonantia and avowals.   (249.6–13)

Then come a couple of additional clues which include all the letters of "heliotrope" first in proper and then in jumbled succession. And there you have it, "old Sem," as pat as ABC.

Apparently, however, Izod has already decided to jilt Glugg and is waiting for "Sunny" to land her. She is merely playing with Glugg's dumbness. In another dance, he is taunted and shunned. They pretend to help him, but they only confuse him, shouting at him to speak. They're not playing fair; it's not cricket—"Not by ever such a lot." She comes to him for the third time, but it is not

clear whether Glugg makes the last three guesses or whether
Izod makes them for him while he "speaks" with gestures.

—Willest thou rossy banders havind?
He simules to be tight in ribbings round his rumpff-
korpff.
—Are you Swarthants that's hit on a shorn stile?
He makes semblant to be swiping their chimbleys.
—Can you ajew ajew fro' Sheidam?
He finges to be cutting up with a pair of sissers and to be
buytings of their maidens and spitting their heads into
their facepails.[28]

The three-times requirement has been met. "Twice
is he gone to quest of her, thrice is she now to him." The
girls rest from their temptings, "and their prunktqueen kilt
her kirtles up and set out. And her troup came heeling,
O," but Glugg is left at a crossroads, not knowing where to
turn. As if by waterwitching ("a fork of hazel") he tries
to decide. The "four," as compass directions, form four
points of a quincunx, betting on his move and jeering at
him (251.1–3). He stands and blinks, thrust from the light
but still heated by the "sourceress." "If he spice east he
seethes in sooth and if he pierce north he wilts in the waist."
He'd like to run, but his legs won't move. They want to
"convert" him to say the word, and he has "wishmarks of
mad imogenation."

As for her, now she could take or leave him. He
would be a good tutor, his intellectuality balancing her
sensuousness. But "let his be exasperated, letters be blowed!
I is a femaline person. O, of provocative gender. U unisin-
gular case." Which is why, near the point of the crossing
of their paths, the twins must fight "for the prize of a
thou."

The struggle is between narcissism ("—Now may Saint
Mowy of the Pleasant Grin be your everglass and even

prospect!") and marriage for Glugg (252.7–13) ("—And may Saint Jerome of the Harlots' Curse make family three of you which is much abedder!") As the twins fight, the "continence" of each is fallen. The girls can't make out which of the two is "artthoudux" and which is "hetero-tropic."[29]

Glugg's pride (as well as his "bride") is gone. He should propose marriage (253.11–16), but, instead, his offer has been to "Come into the garden, Maud." Evidently he has failed for the third time, for she is wearing none of the "colors" he has guessed. No choice between the two merrily fighting boys is ever made, however, because suddenly, in the drama, appears *deus ex machina,* the "largely longsuffering laird of Lucanhof." Where did he come from? It looks like old Joe (254.24), but it's really old Finn (and all his other incarnations) awakened from the earth. (As Joyce says in the introduction of the characters, the twins scrap until they "adumbrace a pattern of somebody else or other.") The producer, in a dramatic pantomime (255.27), causes the Father, like Adam, to sleep, and brings forth the filly-mother (who is also the hen). She collars the pullet and the twins and puts out the fire. It is near lesson-time. Izod, the little cloud girl, who is supposed to go to bed, cannot sleep. She sulks and weeps, because she has been frustrated in her wooing, while her looking-glass "stella" laughs and whispers. The slam of a door—the "thunderword" says "shut the door" in several languages—closes the action. The play is over. Nick (Nek Nekulon) and Mick (Mak Makal) are reconciled (258.10–18). Darkness has descended, the door is closed, and the claims of light and sun, as dramatized in the heliotrope riddle, are temporarily forgotten.

The drama is apparently a prelude of ineffectuality anticipating the type of adult consummation, illustrated earlier in the Prankquean story, which will eventually befall the children. The use of Shem—or Glugg—as the central character in the play, however, indicates that there is more importance attached to the chapter than this. "Heliotrope" is most certainly a figure of speech for the son and that which turns toward the sun. As the answer to a riddle, posed at a "crossroads," it seems at first to be the password for opening the gate to a son-change—in effect, a rebirth—a crossing over into a new cycle of marriage, or fertile sex. The Shem son, however, does not pass, and there is every indication that the angelic Chuff, the Shaun-type son, would not have passed either, for different reasons.[30] In one section of the chapter dealing with HCE's trial (I, iv), there is testimony on the part of Hyacinth O'Donnell, the "mixer and wordpainter" (an alias of the cad and W. P., the Wet Pinter) which pertains to and anticipates Glugg-Shem's failure in the colors game. It is one of the sections to which endless attention could be paid, but I will here be concerned only with the single question and answer pertinent to both the Prankquean and the heliotrope themes. The question: "Lindendelly, coke or skilllies spell me gart without a gate?" The answer: "Harlyadrope" (89.18–19). The similarity of "Lindendelly" to "Londonderry" gives the clue that Joyce is probably, like Swift with his "little language," exchanging "l's" and "r's" in the question, which takes the form of a riddle.[31] One might translate it as "Londonderry, Cork, or Skerry, spare me guilt without a gate," an interpretation which carries an obvious enough reference to infertile sex, if we accept the idea that passing through the door signifies genital consummation. "Gart," however, alludes to a garden (German "garten"). In a garden without a gate, one certainly does no crossing through. And if one gets as far as the garden and cannot "come out" or "go in" through the door, one has failed. Apparently this applies to the Shem-type son. The reason for failure is in the answer, "Hardly a drop"—lack of firewater—in Shem's case the fear of and aversion to anything like total immersion. It is well to recall, though, that Shaun appears to be the sun-son in the colors game,[32] and he—although he demonstrates in the Jaun chapter that he can use as lewd language as Shem—because of his pose of purity is as far from direct sexual involvement as his brother. So, granting that "heliotrope" certainly applies to the sons' "troops"—their privates —and to sexual games sons and "trollops" play before marriage, it is, after all, a dry word, not to be equated, as the proper answer to a riddle dealing with sex, with the wondrous firewater of Finnegan's whisky or the Prankquean's rain. The game, then, is sere mimicry of the green-tea-events of the parents, perhaps because the sons in the dream, being only opposing aspects of their father, are incomplete as human beings. Shaun represents the day-reality, Shem the night-time dream-reality, and Shem has much to teach Shaun about the dark underworld in the next chapter. But neither reality is the total man, and the twins both have a great deal to learn.

Another point which can't be overlooked in this connection is the opposition of "hyacinth" to "heliotrope" as associated with the characteristics of the twins. I have already pointed out that Hyacinth O'Donnell is a Shem-type alias. W.P. (who is really the same person) alludes to Hyacinth's odor (87.12), which immediately connects him with Shem, who was said to be kicked out of his dwelling because of his smell, the scullerymaids holding their noses and remarking "aboon the lyow why a stunk [hyacinth], mister" (181.25–26). (Cf. the girls, in the trial chapter, "stincking thyacinths" through Chuff's curls: 92.16–17.) Shem's "letter" manuscript is a "whyacinthinous riot of blots and blurs" (118.28–29), and Jerry Porter is self-described as a writer of an "anemone's letter" which "I ha'scint ["hyacinth" and "scent," as well as "sent"] for my sweet" (563.16–17). Hyacinth and heliotrope are both purple flowers associated with the twins, but Sunny Shaun, the Hilary of the Prankquean story, is more nearly like the sun-god king (note Prankquean allusions in "hilariohoot of Pegger's Windup": 92.6), and is contrasted with the gloomy Shem, Tristopher of the Prankquean story, who is more closely allied with the rainy mother (cf. "tristitone of the Wet Pinter": 92.7), and with homosexuality, like the mythical Spartan boy whose flower, the hyacinth, bears the words of grief, "Ai, Ai."[33]

What happens in the "Mime" has to do with heterosexuality that reaches no fruitful consummation. The treatment of "heliotrope" expands the theme of the "two" in the park, for it concerns encounters between a boy and a girl. As related to the park episodes, "heliotrope" applies to the "two,"[34] whereas "hyacinth" pertains to the perversion connected with the "three." Both park events, about which the whole world gossips in *Finnegans Wake*, take place on the threshold of a figurative door. (The wall serves as another form of divider between in and out, old and new, etc.) In the waking-up chapter (IV) of the book, these are recalled as "Greanteavvents! Hyacinssies with heliotrollops! Not once fullvixen freakings [*fuldvoksen frøkener* = "fullgrown young ladies" (Danish)] and but dubbledecoys! It is a lable iction on the porte of the cuthulic church and summum most atole for it. Where is that blinketey blanketer, that quound of a pealer, the sunt of a hunt whant foxes good men!" (603.28–32). These two three-part stories, then, by their close relationship to the central park episode, constitute accumulating evidence for the remarkable congruity of form and content in the book. The conviction of that coherence will continue to grow.

3] *The Captain, and the Russian General*

THE FIRST tale told in the pub (II, iii) is extremely difficult to extricate from the carousing and the lewd talk of the "cupstoomerries" in Earwicker's "house of call." The early part of the chapter corresponds to and surpasses in confusion the Circe portion of *Ulysses*. All the topics dealt with so far in *Finnegans Wake* are being discussed and argued by the "Finnfannfawners"; the host has been given a twelve-tube radio through which he listens to the story of the Norwegian captain and the tailor, as well as to advertisements, notices, and weather announcements; he himself, however, often seems to be "their tolvtubular high fidelity daildialler," an "harmonic condenser enginium . . . tuned up by twintriodic singulvalvulous pipelines" (310.1–5) [35] and wired for a permanent connection "up his corpular fruent and down his reuctionary buckling . . . lill the lubberendth of his otological life" (310.17–20). Since his equipment will pick up information from the past, he becomes a broadcasting earwig which wakens listeners by transmitting meaningful tales received in his own "auricular forfickle." "So he sought with the lobestir claw of his propencil the clue of the wickser in his ear" (311.10–11).

The main "program" is the story of the Norwegian captain and the tailor. Although the narrative certainly alludes to Irish history—invasion, Christianization, and race-amalgamation—my own analysis will deal only with the three-times-is-a-charm motif and the sexual implications already under discussion.[36] What happens is that the captain tries to get a pair of trousers (two sirs, the twins) and a doublet (a "singlette" with a looking-glass double) from a male tailor-creator.[37] Naturally, this is impossible, even though the tailor—sometimes one, sometimes three—is described in feminine terms, and "tries" the "suit," or courtship, twice. The attempts to "fit" the captain with the "suit" are homesexual encounters; no woman is involved at first. At one point, the ghost of the Earl of Howth looms, and reminders of his marriage penetrate the perverted atmosphere. The captain and the opposing tailor contend as Shem and Shaun types, sailor against tailor.[38] Eventually, the sailor-captain is grounded and reverses roles with the tailor Kersse, who appears in sailor clothes; the "invader" becomes the native. When the two are reconciled (and turn into Humphrey), a part of the new man is the marrying groom and another part is the father of the bride. But "tailor" now means neither Kersse nor the captain but the three-in-one creator united with the woman.

The telling—or broadcasting—of the tale begins as if it had just been tuned in: "—Then sagd he [the captain] to the ship's husband" (311.21). The captain asks the ship's husband[39]—in language which echoes the Prankquean riddle, "Hwere can a ketch [where can I catch] or hook alive a suit and sowterkins?" (311.22–23).[40] The ship's husband, using cant to give private double meaning to his instructions, asks the tailor, his best friend and bedfellow,[41] to "take and make the captain a suit," but also to "fake an capstan make and shoot" the captain. Since *"fakke"* in Norwegian means "catch" or "nab" and *"make"* means "spouse," the homosexual overtones are clear. Moreover, one can hardly imagine "a peer of trouders under the pattern of a cassack" as a satisfactory fit! The tailor wants to "prove"—or try on—the suit; the captain complies,[42] says a hurried goodbye ("fur whale"), and takes his French leave, without his trousers. The shouting of the ship's husband to "Stolp, tief, stolp, come bag to Moy Eireann!" promises an Irish "Ann," but the captain, like the Prankquean, makes himself absent for "seven sailend sonnenrounders," during which it rains forty days and forty nights, sailing the seas and doing some male "raigning" which threatens not at all the "ryehouse reigner," steward of the "queen of Prancess" whom he, the "ship's husband," would like to keep "as niece as a fiddle" (312.24).

The first encounter is past, and the tale is interrupted by comments, requests for drinks, and sly allusions to the pertinence of the story to the innkeeper himself. The drinkers remind the host of his own "fall" as a humpty-dump-on-a-wall-poor-fool-luderman (the thunder-word, "Bothallchoractorschummingaroundgansumuminarumdrumstrumtruminahumptadumpwaultopoofoolooderamaunsturnup"), and recall, first, his sins in the park and then, in ribald language, his marriage, the conception of the twins, and the birth of his daughter.

As the innkeeper gives the three "tailors" (tale-tellers, those who have been gossiping and jeering) another shot of firewater, the actual scene in the pub merges with the second appearance of the captain in the radio story, for he comes in and surprises from the rear the ship's husband and the "three tailors" in a highly provocative position. A lot of "wetting" takes place in connection with this account of perversion, indicating that a comparison with the Prankquean's micturition is intended (315.9–16). The captain greets the others, asks the whereabouts of his friend, Sulkers or Sutchenson, but gets no answer. The ship's husband and the tailor speak to each other privately in French and then "good mothers gossip" turns to the captain directly and says they had been afraid he was dead and were planning for his wake. The insinuation is that they thought the captain had been too drunk to navigate and had fallen to the bottom of the sea:

> fearsome . . . he had gone dump in the doomering this tide where the peixies would pickle him down to the button of his seat . . . with the help of Divy and Jorum's locquor and shut the door after him to make a rarely fine Ran's cattle of fish.[43] . . . And they laying low for his home gang in that eeriebleak mead, with fireball feast and turkeys tumult and paupers patch to provide his bum end. (316.16–24)

The Norwegian captain orders food and drink, the "shop's housebound" gives orders for him to be served, and the three tailors, muttering how he hadn't complained about the first "suit" ("Nohow did he kersse or hoot alike the suit and solder skins": 317.22), offer "three's here's for repeat of the unium!" (317.29). The solicitor is so intent on his own prominence ("so promonitory himself") that he is "obliffious to the headth of hosth that rosed before him," under the semblance of mortal man. It is the spirit of the Earl of Howth, still "trystfully acape" for the young river he wed. The language changes to memorialize that marriage, which makes a mockery of the present ineffectual "unium." "Should anerous enthroproise call homovirtue, duinnafear! The ghem's to the ghoom be she nere zo zma." But the spectre fades away.

The captain has eaten and has drunk his three swallows of ale in one gulp. The "firewater" gets him all "torched up," and he asks for the tailor: "where's Horace's courtin troopsers?" (Where is "a chara" cutting the trousers—or where are a chara's courting troopers [privates]?) Pukkelson (son of *Pukkel*, or "Hump") has put him behind the "oasthouse." The captain curses the tailor and calls him all the abusive names he can think of, alleging that "he is that woe worstered wastended shootmaker whatever poked a noodle in a clouth!" (320.16–17). So the

second "tryon" is a failure. Again the captain heads for
the high seas, in spite of the "wife's hopesend's" call to
"Come back to May Aileen." He hits storms, and "soaking
scupper, didn't he drain" (320.30–31).

There is an intermission before the third act, which
begins with the appearance of Kersse the tailor in a sailor
suit and a white hat. From off-stage comes a call for him
to "take off thatch whitehat," and there ensues a word
battle (with plenty of fire imagery) between the non-
emerging captain—now called Tersse—and the tailor transformed to a sailor. Kersse defends himself and blames the
captain, who "with his beauw on the bummell," was impossible to "suit": "and there is never a teilwrmans in the
feof fife of Iseland . . . could milk a colt in thrushes foran
furrow follower width that a hole in his tale and that hell
of a hull of a hill of a camelump bakk" (323.19–23).

Again the real scene and the tale are confused, as the
humpbacked innkeeper, ghostlike (323.35–324.1), returns
from his radio-dream (his "uppletoned layir") to the pub
scene. The guests hail him and seize him, as if he were
the elusive captain. The "set" is tuned to another station,
and, in the language of a weather announcement, the Norwegian captain is said to be lost, but predictions are that
he, in his unusable suit of clothes, will return tomorrow
to marry the seamstress.

> As our revelant Colunnfiller predicted in last mount's
> chattiry sermon, the allexpected depression over Schium-
> dinebbia, a bygger muster of veirying precipitation and
> haralded by faugh sicknells, (hear kokkenhovens ekstras!)
> and umwalloped in an unusuable suite of clouds, having
> filthered through the middelhav of the same gorgers' ken-
> nel on its wage wealthwards and incursioned a sotten retch
> of low pleasure, missed in some parts but with lucal driz-
> zles, the outlook for tomarry (Streamstress Mandig)
> beamed brider, his ability good.
> What hopends to they?

Giant crash in Aden. Birdflights confirm abbroaching nubtials. Burial of Lifetenant-Groevener Hatchett, R. I. D. Devine's Previdence. (324.26–325.2)

The "ship's gospfather," a "marriage mixter" (328.4), makes "by my main makeshift . . . one fisk and one flesk" (325.21) of himself and the two a charas[44]—"ahorace," who is now "the husband's capture," the "rude hunnerable Humphrey"; and "aaherra," the "secondnamed sutor," the transformed tailor, "for the two breasts of Banba are her soilers and her toilers" (325.24). The captured groom is baptized "Ocean," "Oscarvaughther," and "Erievikkingr," the "streameress mastress to the sea," although the captain resists the conversion.[45] Kersse is now the "coaxfonder" of Nanny Ni Sheeres, who is to become "a full Dinamarqueza" (Danish countess), "la Charmadouiro, Tina-bat-Talur," and is as much doted upon by her father as "anny livving plusquebelle." She and her husband will do the "tailoring" now: "she will make a suomease pair and singlette, jodhpur smalls and tailorless, a copener's cribful, leaf, bud and berry, the divlin's own little mimmykin puss" (329.1–4). The connection with the ALP-HCE wedding, illustrated in the Prankquean story, is made plain. Her "fresh racy turf is kindly kindling up the lovver with the flu, with a roary-boaryellas would set an Eriweddyng on fire, let aloon an old Humpopolamos with the boomarpoorter on his brain" (327.31–34).

"Cawcaught. Coocaged" (329.13).[46] Like Noah on Mount Ararat, the sailor is grounded. "And it was dim upon the floods only and there was day on all the ground" (330.10–11). "He goat a berth. And she cot a manege. And wohl's gorse mundom ganna wedst" (330.28–29). The door again is shut and procreation begins. "Knock knock. War's where! Which war? The Twwinns. Knock knock. Woos without! Without what? An apple. Knock knock" (330.30–32). Once more, the reign has come to the man, for "the wild main from Borneholm has jest come to crown" (331.35–36) . The inevitable thunderclap ("Pappappapparrassannuaraghheallachnatullaghmonganmacmacmacwhackfalltherdebblenonthedubblandaddydoodled") includes the information that Pappa appears and a new era has naturally begun after the fall. Daddy had doodled, and an unruly person—a male prankster this time—had "creeked a jest." It was "Gestapose to parry off cheekars or frankfurters" from the door (332.5–8) . The union of the three into one, and the third encounter's ending with the woman, are summarized at the close of the tale:

> Such was the act of goth stepping the tolk of Doolin, drain and plantage, wattle and daub, with you'll peel as I'll pale and we'll pull the boath toground togutter, testies touchwood and shenstone unto pop and puma, calf and condor, under all the gaauspices (incorporated) , the chal and his chi, their roammerin over, gribgrobgrab reining trippetytrappety (so fore shalt thou flow, else thy cavern hair!) to whom she (anit likeand please thee!). Till sealump becamedump to bumpslump a lifflebed, (altolà, allamarsch! O gué, O gué!) (332.10–18)

The "trou" story as a "hole" concerns the "twosirs" of the "suit" as they pertain to the door motif. Continuing to be "punny," I think Joyce is concerned with an attempted "breeches" birth through a broken breach due to a false "clothes." I'm not making it up. The evidence accrues throughout the book that the captain and tailor story metaphorically recounts a premarital sin, that of anal homosexuality; the sin represents an imperfect opening and a false closing of the door and results not in fruitful issue but in a breach in a wall which must be mended before a real "wetting" can take place. That the first two encounters of the Norwegian captain with the tailor correspond with the meeting between HCE and the cad in the park, antedating HCE's marriage, is indicated by the fact that, immediately following the summary of the outcome of the story, Joyce writes:

> But before that his loudship was converted to a landshop there was a little theogamyjig incidence that hoppy-go-jumpy Januany morn when he colluded with the cad out on the beg amudst the fiounaregal gaames of those oath-massed fenians for whome he's forcecaused a bridge [breach] of the piers [peace], at Inverleffy, mating pontine of their engagement, synnbildising graters and things, eke ysendt? [not so?] O nilly, not all, here's the first cataraction!   (332.23–29)

And, in a section of the trial testimony (I, iii), a witness called "El Caplan Buycout, with the famous padre's turridur's capecast," sings out, "We have meat two hourly . . . meet too ourly, matadear!" (60.29–31). Walt Meagher, a "naval rating," somehow connected with the breach in the wall, adds a questionably defensive word about the affair as he explains to his fiancee (s), Questa and Puella, "piquante and quoite": "I also think, Puellywally [girl-bridge, plus wall], by the siege of his trousers there was someone else behind it—you bet your boughtem blarneys—about their three drummers down Keysars [Kersse's] Lane (Trite!) " (61.24–27). The too-early incident has made of the defendant an imposter, a pseudo-creator in the pattern of life constantly renewed. The interrogators of Yawn (III, iii) force the latter to describe the false closing of the door and the exposure of the bluffing "groom." Was he

> wearing his cowbeamer and false clothes of a brewer's grains pattern with back buckons with his motto on, *Yule Remember*, ostensibly for that occasion only of the twelfth day Pax and Quantum wedding, I'm wondering.
> —I bet you are . . . I am sorry to have to tell you, hullo and evoe, they were coming down from off him. . . .
> —Ay, another good button gone wrong.
> —Blondman's blaff! Like a skib leaked lintel the arbour

leidend with . . . ? [a skiff sneaked into the harbor laden
with . . . ?]
—Pamelas, peggylees, pollywollies, questuants, quainta-
quilties, quickamerries.   (508.3–20)

Through broken "material," creativity is lost; an abortive
birth—or, more nearly correct, no issue at all—is the result
of perverted sexuality. "A talor would adapt his caulking
trudgers on to any shape at see. Address deceitfold of wovens
weard" (375.34–35) . Before the marriage of "Massa and
Missus," the son goes

> sliding along and sleeting aloof and scouting around and
> shooting about. Allwhichwhile or whereaballoons for good
> vaunty years Dagobert is in Clane's clean hometown prep-
> ping up his prepueratory and learning how to put a broad
> face bronzily out through a broken breached meataerial
> from Bryan Awlining! Erin's hircohaired culoteer.   (274.26–
> 275.2)

The breach caused by such sin and guilt can be mended by
the woman who presents the right door, and of course it is
Anna Livia who says, looking back on the past:

> The folgor of the frightfools is olympically optimominous;
> there is bound to be a lovleg day for mirrages in the open;
> Murnane and Aveling are undertoken to berry that ort-
> chert: provided that. You got to make good that breach-
> suit, seamer. You going to haulm port houlm, toilermaster.
> (613.28–32)

The second tale told in the pub is an endtime story
of "his awebrume hour" (336.14–15). We are to "Leave the
letter that never begins to go find the latter that ever comes
to end, written in smoke and blurred by mist and signed
of solitude, sealed at night" (337.11–14) . The Russian general father-figure is, as a matter of fact, the domesticated

captain, whose demise widows the ex-tailor's daughter. "Don Gouverneur Buckley's in the Tara Tribune, sporting the insides of a Rhutian Jhanaral and little Mrs Ex-Skaerer-Sissers is bribing the halfpricers to pray for her widower in his gravest embazzlement" (375.23–26). Paradoxically, he, as "widower," lives on after *her* departure. The actors in the next drama are the twins, playing the roles of Butt and Taff, soldier-buddies. Whereas the captain and tailor story is one which illustrates rivalry between the brothers, the tale of how Buckley shot the Russian general dramatizes the Oedipal wish of the son (s) to replace the father.

The three phases of the action are not so clearly distinguished as they were in the original anecdote. It was another of John Joyce's stories about an Irish soldier, Buckley, who tried twice to shoot a Russian general in the Crimean War before he actually fired. The first time, he was bedazzled by the general's uniformed splendor; the second time, the general was squatting to defecate, and Buckley's pity for such human helplessness made him lower his gun. But when the general started to wipe himself with a piece of turf, Buckley's respect and pity vanished and he fired. As Glasheen says, "Joyce went on to make the turf Irish and the general insulting Ireland."[47]

The account in *Finnegans Wake* is turned into a vaudeville skit on a TV screen, Taff operating as foil or straight-man for the comedian Butt, who pretends to be recalling a war-time incident of many years ago. But the story is also the narrative of a Freudian drama. Taff sets the Oedipal atmosphere:

> And may he be too an intrepidation of our dreams which we foregot at wiking when the morn hath razed out limpalove and the bleakfrost chilled our ravery! Pook. Sing ching lew mang. Upgo, bobbycop! Lets hear in remember the braise of. Hold! [the days of old]. (338.20–33).

As small boys, appalled to witness the "bigness" of the father, Butt and Taff, in reminiscence, describe the disgusting grandeur of the general.[48]

> BUTT. . . . Sehyoh narar, pokehole sann! [Sayonara, Pukkelson;[49] also refers to the "sight" witnessed.] Manhead very dirty by am anoyato ["Manhead" very dirty boy; I'm annoyed]. (339.2–3)
>
> TAFF. . . . Grozarktic! Toadlebens! Some garmentguy! Insects appalling, low hum clang sin! A cheap decoy! Too deep destroy! Say mangraphique, may say nay por daguerre! (339.21–23)

The father-general is seen when he is stooping to defecate, and Butt describes the genital "tree" and the "warful doon's bothem": "Here furry glunn. Nye? Their feery pass. Tak! With guerillaman aspear aspoor to prink the pranks of primkissies. And the buddies behide in the byre" (340.9–12). The boys have a case against the bigger man, for he defiled the lilies of the field and consorted with the three soldiers (340.22–24). After they dance and sing their complaints, the first and second sports reports are given on the television set, as an interruption to their show, whereupon Taff changes his tactics and brings Butt back to the actual narrative. Butt remembers seeing the general looking for a place to relieve himself ("lyoking for a stooleazy for to nemesisplotsch allafranka and for to salubrate himself with an ultradungs heavenly mass at his base": 343.27–29).[50] Butt says he wanted to "shoot," but because of pity and fear he was unable to: "when I looked upon the Saur of all the Haurousians with the weight of his arge fullin upon him from the travaillings of his tommuck and reuckenased the fates of a bosser there was fear on me . . . and . . . I adn't the arts to" (344.33–345.2).[51] Butt is given the communion cup by Taff, temporarily playing the "foregiver of trosstpassers," and so the first episode passes.

On television, the news broadcasts and commercials

continue, apparently diverting the vaudeville actors at the same time as they divide the attention of the audience and, in addition, contributing to the Freudian pattern. Taff urges that the "ballet" go on. (He already knows the old story; he still functions as straight man: "And don't live out the sad of tearfs, piddyawhick!") Butt again places the action in the deep past, and then proceeds: "But Icantenue." He says he proposed a raid on the enemy, the "dead beats," and, in recalling the good old days with his buddies—now all in Valhalla ("waulholler")—he reveals that he was one of the notorious "three" in the park that day of HCE's much-talked-about crime (348.20–23). Taff goes into a frenzied dance, memorializing those remembered events. Then Butt and Taff do a fade-out, and the television screen presents "the charge of a light barricade" (349.11; the "door"). Reference to the sun-god qualities of Taff and the nighttime character of Butt—reminiscent of the qualities of Chuff and Glugg in the "Mime" episode—is provided in the description of this fade-out and partial merging of the two sons: "In the heliotropical noughttime following a fade of transformed Tuff and, pending its viseversion, a metenergic reglow of beaming Batt" (349.7–9). A "still" emerges, the figure of the Russian general, ghostlike, all his sins—which he now tries to confess—still on him. (The parallels with the three "fathers"—King Hamlet, Polonius, and Claudius—are vague, but undeniable.) But he "cant came back" (349.36), though "there will be a hen collection of him after avensung on the field of Hanar" (350.7–8).

Butt, denying his Oedipal wishes, "tells how when he was fast marking his first lord for cremation the whyfe of his bothem [the wipe of his bottom; the wife of both of them] was the very lad's thing to elter his mehind" (350.13–15). He, after all, had his "billyfell of duckish delights." He brags about all his conquests in those "droomodose days." He also protests that he never cared a thing for men (homosexuality) because he always had those sisters who would never let him down. He never went wrong until he saw the Russian general in all his splendor and sexual power, and then he took his own gun and shot. The episode must be read not only as a symbolic castration but also as a symbolic homosexual union with the father, participated in by both sons (as will be made clear in a later passage which indicates that Butt and Taff became one in the father). It seems expedient, here, to reproduce a long portion of this section, with some explanatory notes, to strengthen these interpretations.

> I was a bare prive without my doglegs but I did not give to one humpenny dump, wingh or wangh, touching those thusengaged slavey generales [genitals; "thusengaged generales" = sexual intercourse] of Tanah Kornalls, the meelisha's deelishas, pronouncing their very flank movements in sunpictorsbosk. Baghus the whatwar! I could always take good cover of myself and, eyedulls or earwakers, preyers for rain or cominations, I did not care three tanker's hoots, ('sham! hem! or chaffit!) for any feelings from my lifeprivates on their reptrograd leanins because I have Their Honours booth my respectables soeurs assistershood off Lyndhurst Terrace, the puttih Misses Celana Dalems, and she in vinting her angurr can belle the troth on her alliance and I know His Heriness, my respeaktoble medams culonelle on Mellay Street, Lightnints Gundhur Sawabs, and they would never as the aimees of servation let me down. Not on your bludger life, touters! No peeping, pimpadoors! And, by Jova, I never went wrong nor let him doom till, risky wark rasky wolk, at the head of the wake, up come stumblebum (ye olde cottemptable!), his urssian gemenal, in his scutt's rudes unreformed and he went before him in that nemcon enchelonce with the same old domstoole story [(Danish) *domstol* = court of justice (here, "judgment seat") ; also defecation "stool"] and his upleave the fallener as is greatly to be petted (whitesides

do his beard!) and I seen his brichashert offensive and his boortholomas vadnhammaggs [Bartholomew Vanhomrigh] vise a vise them scharlot runners and how they gave love to him and how he took the ward from us (odious the fly fly flurtation of his him and hers! [Expresses the Oedipal jealousy of the son.] Just mairmaid maddeling it was it he was!) and, my oreland for a rolvever, sord, by the splunthers of colt [splendor of God] and bung goes the enemay the Percy rally got me, messger, (as true as theirs an Almagnian Gothabobus!) to blow the grand off his aceupper. Thistake it's meest! And after meath the dulwich. We insurrec-tioned[52] and, be the procuratress of the hory synnotts, be-fore he could tell pullyirragun to parrylewis, I shuttm,[53] missus, like a wide sleever! Hump to dump! Tumbleheaver!

TAFF (*camelsensing that sonce they have given bron a nuhlan the volkar boastsung is heading to sea vermelhion but too wellbred not to ignore the umzemlianess of his rifal's preceedings, in an effort towards autosotorisation, effaces himself in favour of the idiology alwise behounding his lumpy hump off homosodalism which means that if he has lain amain to lolly his liking—cabronne! —he may pops lilly a young one to his herth — combrune —*) Oholy rasher, I'm believer! And Oho bullyclaver of ye, bragadore-gun-neral! The grand ohold spider! It is a name to call to him Umsturdum Vonn! Ah, you were shutter reshottus and sieger besieged.[54] Aha race of fiercemarchands counterina-tion oho of shorpshoopers.[55]

BUTT (*miraculising into the Dann Deafir warcry, his bigotes bristling, as, jittinju triggity shittery pet, he shouts his thump and feeh fauh foul finngures up the heighohs of their ahs!*) Bluddymuddymuzzle! The buckbeshottered! He'll umbozzle no more graves nor horne nor haunder, lou garou, for gayl geselles in dead men's hills! Kaptan (backsights to his bared!) , His Cumbulent Embulence, the frustate fourstar Russkakruscam, Dom Allaf O'Khorwan, connundurumchuff.   (351.20–352.34)

Taff, who has been struggling to maintain the illusion that he has had no part in the events just recounted, becomes more and more uneasy in the attempt to smother the guilt rising from the depths of his unconscious. He "has been sulphuring to himsalves all the pungataries of sin praktice in failing to furrow theogonies of the dommed" (352.36–353.1) . The last word in the long passage quoted— "connundurumchuff"—identifies Shaun, in the guise of Chuff, with the commander-in-chief father. The moment of doom is about to annihilate—and consolidate—the three. Butt ambiguously grieves for his father's death and complains that the "general" yet lives (or lives not) : "That he leaves nyet is my grafe" (353.9–10) . He then reenacts the final scene, the shooting which occurred at twelve o'clock sharp and caused the "abnihilisation of the etym" (353.22; the "Word"; atom; time; Atem as father-god) which is repeated around the world and in all eras (353.28–29) . Taff apprehends a shadow moving; Butt, recognizing the ghost of Finn MacCool, becomes faint. He and Taff, "now one and the same person" (354.8) , are "umbraged by the shadow of Old Erssia's magisquammythical mulattomilitiaman" (354.9–10) , and the three become one. The variation on the Quinet passage which follows (354.22–36) says that the "mutthering ivies" and the "murdhering idies" of the "samuraised twimbs" have never succeeded in stopping the reappearance of the flowers and dancing hours and the repetition of the same old story again and again. "So till butagain budly shoots thon rising germinal let bodley chow the fatt of his anger and badley bide the toil of his tubb" (354.34–36) .

"Shutmup. And bud did down well right" (355.8) .

The silence at the end of the story is soon broken by the comments of the pub customers. And the innkeeper host has his homely say. These tales pertain to all of us, he says (355.21–23; 33–36; 356.1–4). "I have just . . . been reading in a (suppressed) book" (356.19–20), he says—the leaves of which have hardly been used to wipe myself (as the Russian general wiped himself with Irish turf)—all about such "action passiom . . . from burst to past" (356.31–33).

> And whilst (when I doot my sliding panel and I hear cawcaw) [56] I have been idylly turmbing over the loose looves leaflefts jaggled casuallty on the lamatory . . . when I . . . enlivened toward the Author of Nature by the natural sins liggen gobelimned [lying limned (tapestried)] theirs before me . . . am entrenched up contemplating of myself, wiz my naked I, for relieving ["reliving" as well as "relieving"] purposes . . . I sometimes, maybe . . . (when I ope my shylight window and I see coocoo) a notion quiet involuptary of that I am cadging hapsnots as at murmurrandoms of distend renations from ficsimilar phases . . . . [Then] I am highly pelaged [pleased; Pelagian (able to save himself by his own efforts)] . . . to see by their loudest reports from my threespawn bottery parts . . . that . . . when I have remassed me . . . after my contractual expenditures . . . I, my good grief, I am, I am big altoogooder. (357.20–22; 357.27–358.3, 10–16).

This funny and charmingly naive description of HCE's natural recovery after defecation, and re-tumefaction after devitalization, is one of the prime sex-defecation symbols of the thematic essence of *Finnegans Wake,* applied at this point to give final meaning to the replacement story of Buckley's shooting the Russian general. HCE, behind his outhouse door, can watch his own bodily parts in action and understand the larger mysteries of life. Joyce's philosophic optimism is continually illuminated on the sexual level by his humorous treatment of such actions of the bodily parts of both man and woman, each part assuming a human name and interacting with the other members of the genital family.

4] The Door

THE WAY in which the four stories just examined complement each other and contribute severally to thematic cohesion can now be summarized. Already evident is the significance of the door as a symbol common to all four episodes. In the Prankquean story, the woman's "piss-word" which opens the gate provokes the man to thunderous creativity: the slamming of the secret door behind which procreation begins. The Jarl himself is said to be the "dour," the "wicket," the "ark of trihump," and the woman seems to be the key. Elsewhere in the book, such a reading is borne out. Issy says of her "latest lad": "Why I love taking him out when I unletched his cordon gate. Ope, Jack and atem! Obealbe myodorers and he dote so" (459.26–27). On the other hand, the male member "comes out" and crosses the threshold of woman herself, whereupon the door is shut. In the geometry lesson (II, ii), mother's "maids-apron" (297.11) is a dividing line which Kev must pass before he can understand the secrets of woman and of life— a sort of goal-line like the one Tristan, as loverchampion, thrusts through to possess Isolde (395.35–396.2). Issy, too, refers to her "apron stage," the "little passdoor" (146.36), which, in one reference to ALP, is incorporated into the name of woman: *Amnis Limina Permanent* (*Omnis*, meaning "all," but also *amnio*: fetal membrane; *limina*: threshold) .[57] Sometimes the crossing of the threshold, then, is the

50

crossing of the female river, and so the door is a "bridge" to genital union between man and woman. Early in the "Study Period" chapter (II, ii), where the "beginnings" are recapitulated, this kind of cross-over describes the quest that results in the beginning of begetting:

> Approach to lead our passage!
> This bridge is upper.
> Cross.
> Thus come to castle.
> Knock.
> A password, thanks.
> Yes, pearse [pierce].
> Well, all be dumbed! [Silence; end of era].
> O really?
> Hoo cavedin [Who became (first draft)] earthwight
> At furscht kracht of thunder.
> When shoo [she], his flutterby,
> Was netted and named.
> Erdnacrusha, requiestress, wake em!
> And let luck's puresplutterall lucy at
> ease!
> To house as wise fool ages builded.
> Sow byg eat. [So beget; so began it. Also alludes to the
>   sow that eats her own farrow: Ireland.]   (262.2–19)

At any rate, the door of the Prankquean is one of marriage, and, as such, it is the sole preoccupation of the Porters: "As keymaster fits the lock it weds so this bally builder to his streamline secret. They care for nothing except everything that is allporterous. *Porto da Brozzo!*" (560.29–32) .

   In the colors game, the door becomes a barrier to the parents' secrets. Chuff guards the gate, without ever experiencing or caring to experience what is behind it (he is too pure), whereas Glugg's every effort to give the password is frustrated. His own door, as has been seen, is obstinately SHUT: he refuses to be "wet." When (as Shem) he takes a "peepestrella" "out of his westernmost keyhole, spitting at

the impenetrablum wetter" (178.27–30), he finds, instead
of the rainbow bridge ("eachway hope") to "true concilia-
tion," the "gun" of "an unknown quarreler who, supposedly,
had been told off to shade and shoot shy Shem should the
shit show his shiny shnout out awhile to look facts in their
face before being hosed and creased (uprip and jack him!)
by six or a dozen of the gayboys" (179.4–8). Dry, except
for his tears ("Did a weep get past the gates of your pride?"
taunts Issy [145.12–13]), Glugg stands impotent before the
formidable door of heterosexual success. Because the children are not ready for replacing the parents, the interven-
tion of the father and mother places the twins and the
daughter behind the still-protective closed doors, putting
an end to the struggle.

In the Norwegian-captain story, the door is at first a
breach in a wall, a break big enough for a perverted union,
but not a legitimate gate. The captain meets the "gayboy"
tailor and commits the sin which corresponds to that of the
one with the three in the park. The wall is obviously associated with both prostitution and homosexuality. A hole in
a wall or a hole in a gate is not the same as a protectively
closed door or a gate to be opened upon the proper solicita-
tion. But "wilde erthe blothoms" and "whispered sins"
(69.3–4) are historically factual. "There was once upon a
wall and a hooghoog wall a was and such a wallhole did
exist" (69.6–8). The gate in front of HCE'S place was "triple-
patlockt on him on purpose by his faithful poorters to keep
him inside probably" (69.25–26), for he did have an "un-
solicited visitor" who blew "in through the houseking's
keyhole to attract attention, bleated through the gale [gate-
hole] outside which the tairor of his clothes was hogcaller-
ing" (70.18–21). This same solicitor threw stones at the
wicket (72.25–28) in the "last stage in the siegings round
our archicitadel" (73.24) which remained intact because of
the protection given it by the woman inside. The captain's

final "citadel" is a cage where he, too, is trapped behind a closed door by reason of his marriage to the tailor's daughter, but he is, at the same time, creatively "tailoring" his progeny, having let fall his "false clothes" and made good that "breachsuit."

There is another aspect of the door which applies to the captain and the tailor story as well as to the account of Buckley's shooting the Russian general. HCE's inn is said to be "aldays open for polemypolity's sake when he's not suntimes closed for the love of Janus" (133.18–19). Janus is the god of portals—of beginnings and endings—a god who has two faces looking in opposite directions. There is an inside and there is an outside to the door of love—two faces —and there are both open and closed positions for the door. Sexual union means a closed door: an ending and a beginning. But when the door is open, the other side of life—war— takes the place of love, and its perpetuation means that contraries are not yet reconciled. Man and woman are at war until the male rushes out, crosses the threshold and takes possession; rivals are at war to win the maid; sailor and tailor battle as pseudo-lovers until, united with the "father," they are captured by the woman; sons shoot the father through an "opening" and the father is "replaced"—even though, behind his outhouse door, he realizes the wonder of recovery and renewal. War is as necessary to life as love. In fact, the closing of the door which signifies sexual love can follow both ingoing, the beginning of new life, and outgoing, the beginning of new conflicts. HCE "catches his check at banck of Indgangd and endurses his doom at chapel exit" (127.28– 29). Humphrey's withdrawing of his member after his final coition with Anna results in a "Closure," with him on the outside, where he must begin the war with the younger woman all over again. People must mind their "hats goan in" (8.9) but will be minding their "boots [associated with both death and soldiering] goan out" (10.22–23). Between

the captain-and-tailor story and the Buckley story of castration and replacement, aged Kate opens the door (333.1–
5) with a message offering fireworks to HCE from his
"missus," but he does not heed the call. "So the katey's
came and the katey's game. . . . And that henchwench
what hopped it dunneth there duft the. Duras" (334.28–30).
The door is shut to herald the shooting drama which illustrates the end of the era of the father's ascendancy. And
after the tales in the pub, Sockerson bounces all the quar-
reling customers out the door, shutting up shop. Inside,
the aging innkeeper drinks the dregs, the "firewater" left
in the bottoms of the glasses and bottles. Outside, the
revellers carry on the same old arguments which will never
be permanently settled.

Besides the firewater-urine power which acts as a
catalyst to explosive elements, there is another of the "natural" processes which occurs in only two of the stories but
is suggested by the conclusion of a third. There is no doubt
about the import of the thunderous defecation in the
Prankquean story; however, in the Yawn chapter (III, iii),
dung is associated with all three of the other episodes in a
confusing manner. The interrogator asks questions of Yawn
concerning "the enemy," Toucher Tom, or "Thim" or
"Tomsky." (All of these variations of "Tom" are aliases
which permit the shifting of the "enemy" role from twin to
Finn to father to captain to Russian general to Earl of
Howth and back to father.) Yawn is asked if he knows
anything "concerning a boy," "a pagany, vicariously known
as Toucher 'Thom' who is. I suggest Finoglam as his habitat" (506.27–29). Yawn answers as if the question were
an impertinent one about his father: "Never you mind
about my mother or her hopitout" (506.32) . ("Hopitout"
for "habitat" is Yawn's distortion of the interrogator's
"Latin": *Inter nubila numbum.*" Throughout the cate-
chism, Yawn constantly hears and interprets words slightly

different from those spoken in the question.) The "boy" is described as a "man of around fifty," a mental defective, thief, drinker, queer. He turns into the homosexual captain. "Is that the fellow?" asks Yawn. "As mad as the brambles he is. Touch him. With the lawyers sticking to his trewser-shins and the swatmenotting on the basque of his beret. He has kissed me more than once, I am sorry to say and if I did commit gladrolleries may the loone forgive it" (507.13–17). There follow the question concerning the "salt son of a century"—whose name "is not really 'Thom' "—about the "false clothes" worn for a "Pax and Quantum wedding," and Yawn's reply that "they were coming down from off him" (507.32–508.10) —that he was like a ship sneaked into the harbor. The subject of the questioning shifts to the sisters, "P. and Q.," "arpists at cloever spilling,"[58] who, it is learned, were "watching the watched watching. Vechers all" (509.2–3). The subject returns to "friend Tomsky, the enemy" and the falling-off clothes, but now the Russianization of "Thom" to "Tomsky" and the word "rooshian" in Yawn's answer indicate that both clothes and dung are referred to:

> Now, retouching friend Tomsky, the enemy, did you gather much from what he let drop? We are sitting here for that.
> —I was rooshian mad, no lie. About his shapeless hat.
> —I suspect you must have been.
> —You are making your thunderous mistake. But I was dung sorry for him too.
> —O Schaum! Not really? Were you sorry you were mad with him then?
> —When I tell you I was rooshiamarodnimad with myself altogether, so I was, for being sorry for him. (509.5–14)

The inference is that the son was jealous of the creative dung and also "mad" about the fact that the captain-general's "hat" was "shapeless." The heliotrope episode and the dry state of the enemy's sexual powers are evoked by the suggestion from the questioner that "this was solely in his sunflower state and that his haliodraping het was why maids all sighed for him, ventured and vied for him. Hm?" (509.21–23). The general's dropping dung, the captain's falling clothes, and the drooping phallus of the sunson seem to correspond. If defecation is to be creative, it apparently needs the cross-fertilization of the female—and this is the reason Joyce "mixturates" his sex. The woman's role is referred to as being other than an eyelash-batting temptation (509.26–27), and then allusions to the Jarl's defecation in the Prankquean story (in a passage quoted earlier: 509.30–36) bring the discussion around to marriage. "How many were married on that top of all strapping mornings," asks the interrogator. And the answer is that Pap was married to "her," but not Tom and all his "wildes" (510.6–12).

The protagonist of all these events is one and the same person at different stages of his life—or one and the same male organ operating in its different roles as guilty fornicator and sodomist, Oepidal castrator and perpetrator of incest (61.28–29), creative father of children and of "poetry." Premarital pranks with prostitutes are no doubt included in the Prankquean story: homosexuality abounds in both the captain-and-tailor and the Buckley stories; Oepidal wishes pervade the "Mime" episode (where the parents remain preeminent over both chastity and impotence) and also the Buckley drama, in which the childish wish to replace the father is at first defeated by counteracting father-love, then takes the form of symbolic castration and a three-in-one union of the new man. The creator, both landsman and waterman, produces not only human offspring but also literature. His phallus is the pen (for which the woman furnishes the Pee) and is also the letter (T) created for all men to read.

O ferax cupla [fruitful cup; happy fault]! Ah, fairypair! The first exploder [explorer; defecator] to make his ablations in these parks was indeed that lucky mortal which the monster trial showed on its first day out. What will not arky paper, anticidingly [ludicrously (antic; prank)] inked [linked] with penmark, push, per sample prof, kuvertly falted [folded; faulted], when style [phallic pen; literary style], stink [defecation; ink] and stigmataphoron [stigma; stigmata; metaphor; phallic pistil] are of one sum in the same person? He comes out of the soil very well after all just where Old Toffler is to come shuffling alongsoons Panniquanne starts showing of her peequuliar talonts. Awaywrong wandler surking to a rightrare rute [a wrong-way wanderer with a wand, seeking (lurking) a right (rear) route (rut)] for his plain utterrock sukes [sucks; suits], appelled to [appealed; called to; named] by her fancy claddaghs [fancy-clad duds; das (Irish: fathers); clatters. "Cladagh" is also a ring made in the Galway area.] You plied that pokar, gamesy, swell as aye did, while there were flickars [girls (Danish)] to the flores. He may be humpy, nay, he may be dumpy but there is always something racey about, say, a sailor on a horse [*double entendre*]. As soon as we sale [sail; saw; sell] him geen [going; going in] we gates [door; gets] a sprise [price; surprise]! He brings up tofatufa [tauftauf: male "baptism" of woman; also "turf"] and that is how we get to Missas in Massas [mische mische: female "baptism"]. The old Marino Tale. 606.23–607.1)

Such a passage, demonstrating linguistic allusions to every other passage we have looked at so far, prefigures the amazing relatedness of all elements of *Finnegans Wake* and indicates the necessity for a configurational point of view in understanding this book. The same pattern is repeated and added to, again and again, until the nebular mass begins to take a universal shape.

2

THE LETTER

5] T

A FAIR PORTION of the critical discussion of *Finnegans Wake* among Joycean scholars has consisted in speculation regarding the significance of several terms whose phonic affinity should, it seems to me, be a clue to their symbolic relationship; the understanding of these terms will, perhaps, pin down the meaning of that elusive "letter." Consonance and assonance, plus the familiar punning quality so typical of Joyce, constitute grounds for suspicion that "three," "tea," "tree," and even "the" are all closely associated with the tripartite aspect of the letter "T," and that the examination of each of these terms will lead to a recognition of that capital letter as a major symbol of the book. Moreover, the sexual "T," rising and falling as it does throughout the novel, becomes a paradoxical token of man's looming importance—and yet his pitiful impotence—as the power historically represented by a father-god.

I have already argued (in Part One) that the male trio of the Prankquean story are composite parts of the whole man, and that the Jarl "is the two-branched tea tree with dead leaves that must be wet by woman to become rejuvenated." I also suggested that this story illustrated Joyce's method of using the whole to represent the parts. To be more explicit, Joyce's five characters can be regarded as representing members of the propagating family, namely the penis and the testicles on the male side, and the labia of the vulva on the female side. Indeed, I am convinced it would be proper to say that the universe of *Finnegans Wake*, which is, from one point of view, as boundless as infinity, could also be reduced, from another point of view, to the area immediately surrounding and encompassing the human genitals.

Joyce begins in the early pages of *Finnegans Wake* to prepare us for the acceptance of the phallus as a rising three-headed letter ("threehatted ladder") [1] with its "head in thighs under a bush" (89.31), as well as a farewell "letter" ("tata of a tiny victorienne, Alys, pressed by his limper looser": 57.28–29). More than half of the "lines" of this "capitaletter" (397.29) "run north-south . . . while the others go west-east . . . for, tiny tot though it looks . . . it has its cardinal points for all that" (114.3–7) .[2] Its "cardinal" or principal (and crimson) "point" belongs to the father in the center, and the east-west crossing of the sons —"Such crossing [of the T] is antechristian [anti- as well as ante-] of course" (114.11) —forms a "twohandled umberella" (530.29) which is the "gun" (the "twohangled warpon": 615.19) of the composite male. The soldier-privates, then, can be viewed, on the one hand, as the three-in-one emblem of self-guilt which pertains to hidden, partly-forgotten sexual sins not only attached to an individual's past but also inseparable from man's collective memory of original sin. The enemy-accusers are his own genitals (Latin *testes* = witnesses), for he is never free of their insistent presence, continually "playing milliards with his three

golden balls, making party capital [capital T(ea) party]
out of landed self-interest" (589.7–9).

When we can accept the numerous references to male
triads as allusions to the sexual "T," it is easy to understand why, when Margareena is "very fond of Burrus but,
alick and alack! she velly fond of chee" (tea; cheese), she

> complicates the position while Burrus and Caseous are con-
> tending for her misstery by implicating herself with an
> elusive Antonius, a wop who would appear to hug a per-
> sonal interest in refined chees [she's] of all chades [shades]
> at the same time as he wags an antomine art of being rude
> [root; rut] like the boor [boar].

For, as the professor goes on to explain, "This Antonius-
Burrus-Caseous grouptriad may be said to equate the *qualis*
equivalent with the older socalled *talis* on *talis* one"
(166.30–167.5). The three-in-one "tail," variously referred
to as "that hist subtaile [whispered tale; heisted-up tail]
of schlangder" (270.15), the mysterious "teerm" signifying
"majestate" (478.11–12), "thass withumpronouceable tail"
(479.9), that "tag tucked. Up" (315.26) of the Norwegian
captain, ALP's "funnyman's functions Tag" (590.29), becomes the peculiar postscript of the "untitled mamafesta
memorialising the Mosthighest" (104.4) ;[3] thus, in effect,
it is a "teatimestained terminal (say not the tag, mummer,
or our show's a failure) " (114.29–30) appended to a larger
self. In other words, the letter "T" as a postscript stands
in the same relation to the secret communication of the
manifesto as the male genitals do to man, the understanding of whom is every bit as difficult as the deciphering of
the meaning of the mamafesta or the larger communication of *Finnegans Wake* itself. The "T," as the male sexual
member, is not only a symbol for the three-in-one man; it
is also a three-part microcosm of the larger frame of man
which fits so neatly on the form of a cross, and so the sym-

bol "memorializes" (remembers the dead, but also keeps alive the spirit) the "man" which embodied the concept of Christian trinity.[4] Therefore, "tag" or "tail" suggests caricature and decay, the "burnt out ends" of greater days—illustrated by the ass which tags behind the four ludicrous evangelists and reminds grotesquely of a once-majestic burden. The "new man" is "old"—a lover of young girls. But, even at eighty-one, the old codger has a

> daarlingt babyboy *bucktooth*, the thick of a gobstick. . . .
> That why all parks up excited about his *gunn*fodder. . . .
> That why he, *persona erecta*, glycorawman arsenicful *femorniser*, for a trial by julias, in celestial sunhat, with *two purses* agitatating his *the*opot with wokklebout shake. . . .
> And, to make a long stoney badder and a whorly show a parfect sight, his *Thing* went the w*holy*way retup *Suffrogate* Strate. (242.8–24; italics mine)

The double references to the performance of the sexual trinity and the holy suffering of the divine man certify the profane relationship, symbolized by the T-cross, which Joyce unquestionably intended.

That he also intended partly to conceal such a relationship is evident from his use of the intricately decorated *Book of Kells* as an analogue to his own "new testament." The embellishment of language which distinguishes Joyce's final novel from any other work of prose hitherto published serves to weave marvelously involved filaments of camouflage over subjects which, to a defiant anti-Catholic, were still embarrassingly taboo in his own conscience. As Atherton has said, the *Book of Kells* is mysteriously sinful, a "book of kills" (482.33); it has "French leaves" and "obscene pages" and was written by a "writer of calumnies"[5] (Joyce's word: "Calomnequiller," 50.9). It is, moreover, "a very sexmosaic of nymphosis in which . . . Oriolopos . . . persequestellates his vanessas from flore to flore" (107.13–

18) . Joyce makes use, particularly, of the Tunc page of the *Book of Kells* and the capital "T" which begins the Latin inscription, "Tunc crucifixerant XPI cum eo duos latrones" ("Then were there crucified with Him two thieves") . The middle shaft of the initial "T" is a large, curled, serpent-like figure, its base turning into a head out of whose mouth spews twisted, worm-like progeny. The two sides of its upper crossing develop into legs—on the right the two straight fore-paws, resisting the border design encountered by their outstretching, and on the left the downward-curving hind-paws, around and through which a three-pronged tail is entangled, itself a miniature "T." (See frontispiece.) Joyce saw his genital family represented on this Tunc page: the three-part "Big Whiggler" "T" at the top and the double-triangled female symbol ("Tunc" letters jumbled) [6] at the bottom. "It follows that, if the two antesedents be bissyclitties and the three comeseekwenchers trundletrikes, then, Aysha Lalipat behidden on the footplate, Big Whiggler restant upsittuponable, the NCR presents to us . . . an ottomantic turquo-indaco of pictorial shine by pictorial shimmer" (284.22–28).[7] ALP's triangles, in the form of a quincunx on the page, are also referred to as a kiss: "and then that last labiolingual *basium* might be read as a *suavium*" (122.31–32) . The two letters—"T" and "X"—inspired the numerous references to the postscript of the famous *Finnegans Wake* letter: the "T" is the "cruciform postscript from which three *basia* or shorter and smaller *oscula* have been overcarefully scraped away" (122.20–22) and the "X," with "lines of litters slittering up and louds of latters slettering down" (114.17–18) , is the kiss corresponding to the one from lips which have the "keys to. Given" on the last page of *Finnegans Wake*. Although most scholars believe that Joyce was claiming his letter to have been the inspiration for the Tunc page— "plainly inspiring the tenebrous *Tunc* page of the Book of

Kells" (122.22–23)—one cannot overlook the fact that elsewhere in *Finnegans Wake* the debt to the earlier manuscript is owned—"I've read your tunc's dimissage" (298.7) —and the "dimness" of the true meaning of that page was a model for the obscurity surrounding the new gospel according to Joyce. "So, bagdad, after those initials falls and that primary tainctúre," we may go on to examine the meaning of the hen's letter, which was dug up like the buried *Book of Kells* and is a reconstruction (with changes!) of a lost communication.

In connection with the letter in *Finnegans Wake*, Atherton recounts the story of Isis and Osiris from the Egyptian *Book of the Dead*. After Set had murdered Osiris, had dismembered his body and dispersed the pieces, Isis, Osiris' wife, searched until she had found all parts of the body except the male member. To substitute for this deficiency, she formed a new model of the penis and, after piecing the whole body together, conceived Horus, who, when grown, avenged Osiris' horrible death by castrating the murderer, Set. Joyce refers to these events in one of the titles of ALP's manifesto, "How to Pull a Good Horuscoup even when Oldsire is Dead to the World" (105.28–29)[8] which alludes to the neat trick of conception by means of a counterfeit "engine," the idea of a successful coition with an old man already considered "dead" for purposes of propagation, and the idea of vengeance wrought upon the murderer of the father-god by the producing of a new son. The hen, digging up the letter, is apparently rescuing something no longer reconstructable in its original wholeness— something which needs *her* for its recomposition, for its recovered ability to function in a way analogous to its former activity even though it must depend upon an adulterated form. (The last part of the analogy—the vengeance theme—will be dealt with under the discussion of the "the" or dismembered "theos.")

The first version of the letter is certainly fragmented, and in its "grotesquely distorted" condition it is called "masses of meltwhile horse," the result of the melting while drying of the "negative of a horse," or, in plainer words, a horse's ass (111.27–30). For one thing, then, the letter resembles a dried turd, and is appropriately found in a dung-hill type of midden. But this resemblance is only a confusing beginning. We must follow the hen and learn more. "Lead, kindly fowl! They always did: ask the ages" (112.9). Before we get to the bottom of the matter we will see her renewing capacities, for

in her genesic field it is all game and no gammon; she is ladylike in everything she does and plays the gentleman's part every time. . . . Yes, before all this has time to end the golden age must return with its vengeance. Man will become dirigible [directed toward a particular point], Ague [the stiff blue gentian flower] will be rejuvenated, woman with her ridiculous white burden will reach by one step sublime incubation, the manewanting human lioness with her dishorned discipular manram will lie down together publicly flank upon fleece. (112.15–23)

The numerous allusions to the resurrection of the organ of propagation, in connection with the unearthing of the letter, cannot be missed. "He" is her "cock," and

All schwants [she wants; also *Schwantz* (German) and *Svans* (Danish): tail] (schwrites) ischt tell the cock's trootabout him. . . . He had to see life foully the plak and the smut, (schwrites). There were three men in him [referring to his three-in-one organ, his union with his sons, and also to his sodomy] (schwrites). Dancings (schwrites) was his only ttoo feebles [own little *faibles*; only two weaknesses]. With apple harlottes. And a little mollvogels. Spissially (schwrites) when they peaches [two references to urination]. Honeys wore camelia paints [*Honi soit qui mal y pense*]. Yours very truthful. Add dapple inn [A double-N: A-N-N]. (113.11–18)

The *contents* of the letter consist of man's history of sexual (and other resulting) sins and his fall deriving therefrom. The "envelope" (or form), however, is just as important, and the two must be "contemplated simultaneously."[9]

There may be two of us contemplating this letter, continues the narrator of the "Hen" chapter, who "cannot say aye to aye" or "cannot smile noes from noes. Still" (114.1–2), the outward form must be familiar to all. (Here is inserted the description of the letters "T" and "X" on the Tunc page, referred to earlier.) What it means is not yet clear, although the narrator offers some spontaneous guesses at 116.7–10 as to what its fragments might stand for. It is bound to be difficult and ambiguous, to cover its lewdness, for bed language can't be preached by dignitaries any more than long, scholarly words can be grunted by low life (116.25–35). But, whatever it is, it's an "olold stoliolum" (117.10–11) and is told in sounds and signs of "anythongue athall" (117.15–16) in order to have universal application. Even if we doubt the sense and have trouble deciphering it, we can rest assured that it *was written*. "Somebody . . . wrote it, wrote it all, wrote it all down, and there you are, full stop" (118.12–14). We ought to be thankful we even have a "scrap of paper at all to show for ourselves, tare it or leaf it . . . after all that we lost and plundered of it" and we should "cling to it as with drowning hands, hoping against hope all the while that . . . things will begin to clear up a bit one way or another" (118.33–119.6). The "ambiembellishing," however, becomes more and more perplexing; the letter is a confusion of symbols and signs artfully but maddeningly juxtaposed and intertwined (119–122). However, the postscript consists of comparatively simple signs, which do arouse our curiosity (and our senses) so that we can't help but "press on hotly to see the vaulting feminine libido of those interbranching ogham sex upandinsweeps sternly controlled and easily repersuaded by the

uniform matteroffactness of a meandering male fist"
(123.7–10).

There follow various allusions to an earlier manuscript of this letter, a "bestteller popularly associated with
the names of the wretched mariner (trianforan deffwedoff
our plumsucked pattern shapekeeper) " (123.23–25). The
persons represented in the postscript of the letter (the
"Tiberiast duplex": 123.30–31) can be and have been identified. And, whereas the more "original document," like the
Tunc page, "showed no signs of punctuation of any sort"
(Cf. Molly's "postscript" monologue), "this new book of
Morses responded most remarkably to the silent query of
our world's oldest light" (123.33–36). It is "deeply religious
by nature and position, and warmly attached to Thee, and
smearbread and better and Him and newlaidills" (124.12–
14). By comparing the letter with the four-part gospel, and
by putting "two and two together" (124.26), thinkers have
"separated modest mouths" (124.28) in connection with
this letter. "So be it. And it was. The lettermaking of the
explots of Fjorgn Camhelsson when he was in the Kvinnes
country with Soldru's men" (124.28–30) .[10]

So far as the narrator is concerned, the identities involved in the letter ought to pose no more problems. And
there really is "small need after that" to ask riddles concerning the writer of the mess, riddles like "shoots off in
a hiss, muddles up in a mussmass and his whole's a dis-
mantled noondrunkard's son" (125.1–2). "Diremood is the
name is on the writing chap of the psalter" (125.6–7) and
he is "wanted for millinary servance to olderly's person"
(125.10–11). That's why all the girls are out looking for
him. He should be easily recognized; he was "formelly con-
founded with amother. . . . And uses noclass billiardhalls
with an upandown ladder" (125.11–14). To everyone's re-
lief, this writer has dropped the Jesuit and scholarly half
of his nature and is now "that odious and still today insuf-

ficiently malestimated notesnatcher . . . Shem the Penman"
(125.21–23). (Of course, the other half still lives on in
Shaun.)

The story told in the letter is sexual; the letter itself
is a sexual communication somehow connected with the
four gospels; the postscript presents a sexual trinity, with
kisses from a feminine addition to the godhead. And all
womankind waits for her mail since Biddy Doran rescued
that male "T" from the theological dungheap. "Heavenly
twinges," says Issy, "if it's one of his [letters] I'll fearly
feint as swoon as he enterrooms" (278, n.4) . For

> all the world's in want and is writing a letters. A letters
> from a person to a place about a thing. And all the world's
> on wish to be carrying a letters. A letters to a king about
> a treasure from a cat. When men want to write a letters.
> Ten men, ton men, pen men, pun men, wont to rise a
> ladder. And den men, dun men, fen men, fun men, hen
> men, hun men wend to raze a leader. Is then any letters-
> day from many peoples, Daganasanavitch?   (278.13–23)

The passage suggests the importance of sex in history, city-
building, war, and plain survival. Are there any letters
today from any people? Hope and inevitability are both
in the question, and Joyce's letter is an extremely difficult
one because one must accept it as it is, scrapped, mutilated,
rescued from a dungheap, and patched imperfectly. Issy
apologizes for her little letter to the pseudo-divine Jaun,
"this lost moment's gift of memento nosepaper which I'm
sorry . . . is allathome I with grief can call my own but all
the same, listen, Jaunick, accept this witwee's mite, though
a jenny-teeny witween piece torn in one place from my
hands in second place of a linenhall valentino with my
fondest and much left to tutor. X.X.X.X." (457.33–458.3) .
And the return-mail (returning male, like the expected
Jaun) is all that the perennial woman has to look for.

"Madges Tighe, the postulate auditressee, when her dare-mood's a grownian, is always on the who goes where, hoping to Michal for the latter to turn up with a cupital tea [capital "T"] before her ephumeral [funeral (of the father) ; ephemeral existence] comes off without any much father" (369.30–33). The male is her growing son, her dying father and her sexual letter, and she must keep the letters coming for the survival of the race. Religious—or anti-religious—implications come tumbling forward. But, before seizing hold of these inferences for the purpose of a dubious leap of faith (or profanation), two more terms must be considered.

6] *Tree*

THERE CAN be little doubt that the "tree" and "stone" motif which threads through all the chapters of *Finnegans Wake* pertains to the sons, that the tree-stone combination is signified by the "Tristan" spelling of Tristram,[11] and that this dual threat to the old man eventually results in the father's replacement. And, since the three (father and sons) have already been defined as figuratively represented by the phallic "T," there is a strong temptation to suspect that "tree" and "stone" are names for the testicles on either side of the penis, or that "tree" is penis and "stone" is testicle. As a matter of fact, certain passages do support at least the former hypothesis. The end of the Norwegian Captain story, for instance, describes the unified family as pulling the boat together ("we'll pull the boath toground togutter") and refers to the five as "testies touchwood and shenstone unto pop and puma . . . to whom she (anit likenand pleasethee!) " (332.12–17) . The whole story, elsewhere, is referred to as "the tale of a Treestone with one Ysold" (113.18–19) . In one possible reading, tree-stone signifies the amalgamation of the twins as the young Tristan, and links them with the eternal temptress, Isolde.[12] In another reading, tree and stone as the two sons accompany the one who is old, the father: the tale (tail) of the two (tree-stone) plus one ("with one") is old. If one could accept this analogy, the puzzle of shifting the Tristan role from one twin to the other would be solved. Nevertheless, I do not believe that the tree-stone relationship is fully explained by such an interpretation. I am convinced that the branches of the "T" not only swing from side to side but also mark the division between front and rear. There is multiple evidence that "stone" refers to the homosexual rear of the man, and that "tree" is another phonic member of the group signifying the three-pronged "T" in front. As parts of the tree-phallus, the twins are sometimes referred to as leaves or twigs. Shaun, in one place, describes himself as the "most winning counterfeuille on our incomeshare lotetree" (191.17–18), whereas, in the "games" chapter (II, i), the "treegrown girls, king's game . . . are in such transfusion just to know twigst timidy twomeys, for gracious sake, who [of the twins] is artthoudux from whose heterotropic" (252.18–21).

Glasheen tells us that in all Celtic languages the word for "letters" is also the word for "tree." And in *Finnegans Wake*, Joyce's umbrella-shaped tree is spoken of as a rescued piece of wood which, in context, is hardly differentiated from the "word."

> On Umbrella Street where he did drinks from a pumps a kind of workman, Mr Whitlock, gave him [the sinner in the park] a piece of wood. What words of power were made fas between them, ekenames and auchnomes, *acnomina ecnumina*? . . . Batty believes a baton while Hogan hears a hod yet Heer prefers a punsil shapner and Cope and Bull go cup and ball. . . . The war is in words and the wood is the world. (98.24–35)

The passage is a parody of John 1:1. "In the beginning was the Word, and the Word was with God, and the Word was God." (Cf. "the wood that Jove bolt, at his rude word": 80.28.) To understand and relate this discussion to what follows later in the chapter, one must keep in mind the

Word as precreation *Logos*.[13] The "wood" as "word" and as "the world" is another symbolic indication of the author's intention for *Finnegans Wake*. The "word," for which the phallic "T" is the capital letter, presents the key to the kingdom of life. In Joyce's novel, that life is incorporated in the man who represents our "lifetree, our fireleaved loverlucky blomsterbohm, phoenix in our woodlessness, haughty, cacuminal, erubescent (repetition!) whose roots they be asches with lustres of peins" (55.27–30). The tree was planted in the "live-side" of the woman-river,[14] rose as magnificently and miraculously as Jack's beanstalk,[15] bore fruit,[16] and was felled and memorialized.[17]

The most convincing documentation of the father-phallus as "tree" occurs in the chapter of *Finnegans Wake* commonly referred to as the third "watch" of Shaun, where the four "claymen clomb together to hold their sworn starchamber quiry" (475.18–19) of Yawn. The description of this "overlisting eshtree," an analogue of the three-rooted Yggdrasil of Norse mythology which supports the whole universe, significantly follows the wild climax in the inquisition where the questioners are about to discover the "key" to the secrets surrounding the giant-father and are seemingly frustrated by a confusion of lamenting voices and a sudden breakdown in communication. First, we should get an over-all view of Book III. We have to remember that, according to Joyce's letter to Harriet Weaver,[18] the so-called "watches" of Shaun (probably all of Book III) reverse historical time, so that they become "a description of a postman travelling backwards in the night through the events already narrated." The movement "in the night" is accomplished through the framework of a dream (announced at the opening of III, i) ; the father, lying beside his "Anastashie," takes the form of the ass, in his dream, and envisions a new Christ, Shaun the Post. III, i is the part of the dream concerning the future, a wish-fulfillment of the father. III, ii, going back in time, shows Shaun in the role of preacher-Christ, and relates his profane "ascension," which includes his promise of a "comforter" (the Holy Ghost) in the form of his brother, Dave the Dancekerl,[19] and his introduction of the "church," Judia Bride.[20] III, iii, for the purpose of this discussion of the life-tree, can be divided into stages historically preceding the era of the church. The shattering climax, just referred to, uses images of the crucifixion to present a new version of the Fall: that of God Himself, the Christian "father" of mankind. Again remembering that we move backwards, we can read FW 499 and 500 in reverse. On FW 500 occur distorted scraps of diction derived from the crucifixion and resurrection stories: the hopes of the followers that oppression might be crushed; hosannas to the saviour; farewell to the "bride"; the betrayal; the murderous cries of the mob; the march to the cross; the cry of the dying God to the Father ("My God, my God, why hast Thou forsaken me?"); the commitment of the Mother to the care of a new son; and, through it all, the weight of sin on the dying God.[21] These fragments are preceded, on page 499, by what actually followed in time: the earthquake, the descent from the cross, and the keening "wake" which was ended by the resurrection of the god-giant, now referred to as "Funnycoon's Wick."

Having read the record of the slaughter of the Christian God—and setting aside, for a moment, the implications of the "resurrection"—we can now advance to another stage: a pre-Christian version of the fall—that of the life-tree which was the "grawndest crowndest consecrated maypole in all the reignladen history of Wilds. . . . For we are fed of its forest, clad in its wood, burqued by its bark and our lecture is its leave. The cran, the cran the king of all crans. Squiremade and damesman of plantagenets, high and holy" (503.33–504.2). We are envisioning this tree where it "used to be . . . stuck up" (503.30) , in a "place fairly exspoused to the four last winds" (503.18).[22] It stood "foreninst us" not only in "Summerian sunshine" but also in "Cimmerian shudders" (504.5–7; shut doors, as well as showers) . It is called the "ouragan of spaces," a "preeminent giant, sir Arber" (504.14–16) , and then is described as preceding the creation of man and woman, in that it incarnated both sexes, a "mushe, mushe of a mixness" (505.20) . This "shrub of libertine," however, fell and turned to stone.[23] The fall of the tree is now associated with all fall legends, including the angels' fall from heaven, the temptation and fall of Adam through Eve, and the various kinds of capitulation recounted in *Finnegans Wake* (e.g., the record of HCE's fall in the park, the Prankquean story, the Captain and tailor story, and the Russian-general anecdote) .

> —Upfellbowm [Baum = tree; Apfel = apple].
> —It reminds of the weeping of the daughters?
> —And remounts to the sense arrest.
> —The wittold, the frausch and the dibble! How this looseaffair brimsts of fussforus! And was this treemanangel on his soredbohmend because Knockout, the knickknaver, knacked him in the knechtschaft?
> —Well, he was ever himself for the presention of crudities to animals for he had put his own nickelname on every toad, duck and herring before the climber clomb aloft, doing the midhill of the park, flattering his bitter hoolft with her conconundrums. He would let us have the three barrels. Such was a bitte too thikke for the Muster of the hoose so as he called down on the Grand Precurser who coiled him a crawler of the dupest dye and thundered at him to flatch down off that erection and be aslimed of himself for the bellance of hissch leif.   (505.29–506.8)

The tree is now referred to as the *man*—not just the human father of mankind, but also the symbol for man, the phallus.

—Woe! Woe! So that was how he became the foerst [first; forest] of our treefellers? [three fellows; and both the feller and the tree]

—Yesche and, in the absence of any soberiquiet, the fanest [finest; fane-est (fane = archaic word for temple or church)] of our truefalluses [falls; phalluses].   (506.15–18)

Now, although the story of the felling of the ash-tree seems to be merely another recapitulation of the kind of fall described in Christian imagery earlier, I think that its chronological placement in this backward-moving chapter suggests a difference. The legend of the world-ash is supposed to antedate the Biblical fall-myth, which, it will be remembered, was presented as incorporating the crucifixion story—or the "fall" of the God-man, Jesus Christ. The inquisition has reached a depth below the records of Christianity, fragments of which were encountered and passed at a certain stage during the excavation into the archetypal memories of Yawn's midden-heap mind. In the next part of the chapter, the dreamer, having delved to the bottom of the historical dump, can view man as a "truefallus" whose natural rises and falls require no theological explanation. In the beginning was the wood-word, the Here-Comes-Everybody tree.

Where. Cumulonubulocirrhonimbant heaven electing, the dart of desire has gored the heart of secret waters and the poplarest wood in the entire district is being grown at present, eminently adapted for the requirements of pacninc-stricken humanity and, between all the goings up and the whole of the comings down and the fog of the cloud in which we toil and the cloud of the fog under which we labour, bomb the thing's to be domb about it so that . . . it is felt that one cannot with advantage add a very great deal to the aforegoing by what . . . follows, just mentioning however . . . to remind us how, in this drury world of ours, Father Times and Mother Spacies boil their kettle with their crutch. Which every lad and lass in the lane knows. Hence. (599.25–600.4)

HCE, sinner, warrior, city-builder, and husband-father, emerges, in the final part of the chapter, as the old-new man who replaces all heroes and giants and gods, and so we have come to the end of the retrogressive journey and can look at the parents in bed (the Porters, III, iv) [24] from several new points of view. This particular dream is over. "Tableau final. Two me see. Male and female unmask we hem. . . . After having drummed all he dun. . . . Ring down. While the queenbee he staggerhorned blesses her bliss for to feel her funnyman's functions Tag. Rumbling" (590.23–29) .

7] *Tea*

WE SHOULD now be able to interpret one other symbol, belonging to the T-group, which may have been baffling heretofore: the tea that appears in stains, in spoons, in cups, in pots, at parties and wakes—dry or wet, brewed or spilled. Two things are certain: it pertains to both sex and micturition, and it belongs to the discussion of both fruitful and unfruitful union. It is, of course, allied with the capital "T" postscript of the letter. The signature is said to be a "tache of tch"; "tache" is French for "stain," and the Cantonese word for tea ("ch'a") is united with the "T" in "tch." Sexual implications are provided in context by subtle references to tail and spout ("overcautelousness"; "spout of the moment") , and the association with micturition is also ensured by the spelling out of "pee ess" (111.18–22). Elsewhere, the double (male and female) relationship is brought out in such phrases as "Homo Capite [cupo'-tea] Erectus, what price Peabody's money" (101.12–13) and "the souffsouff blows her peaties up and a claypot wet for thee" (117.17–18) . The P(ee) and the T(ea) are letters so important that they supplement the conventional alphabet in at least two places in the *Wake*: In the list of Issy's twenty-eight "classbirds," twenty-six of the names go from "A" to "Z" and the last two girls are named "Phoebe" and "Thelma" (147.14–15) ; again, during the children's games, the "prettimaid tints" are listed from "A" to "Z,"

and are followed by "philomel" and "theerose" (248.2).[25]
Tea undoubtedly refers to a kind of mutual fertility connected with the sexual act.[26] Teatime is bedtime; "bedtime,
teatime," is a note in the *Scribbledehobble* notebook, p.
178. "Teasetime" (FW 191.28) is teaparty time for two.
The word "mamafesta" for the letter, and its association
with the Boston teaparty, connects two-party play with the
"cupital tea" letter that signifies the male reproductive
organ, and the "Tea for Two" theme winds in and out of
many pages of *Finnegans Wake*.[27] Moreover, "Maggy's tea"
(116.24) as a variant of "majesty" must refer to the male
counterpart of the woman—the teaparty king belonging to
Mag—or, in other words, "the senior king of all, Pegger
Festy" (90.36–91.1; Peg, her [Peg's] teaparty king).[28]
Woman is sometimes referred to as the teapot (e.g. 221.13),
but more often she is the firewater-tea that wets or does not
wet the "weapon." "Will ye nought would wet your weap-
ons, warrior bard?" invites Issy (277,n.3). And ALP's cry
that "you never wet the tea!" (585.31) does not refer so
much to unsuccessful copulation as it does to the lost ability of the pair to propagate; both fail to produce the life–
giving fluid; the tea–tree is dry. Her telling him to "go
rightoway back to your Aunty Dilluvia, Humprey, after
that" means that their own cycle is over; it is time for replacement–renewal—the new beginning of the old story.
Tea, then, is not only female urine but is also male semen
which the man "spills" by teaspoonful from his fertile
tree.[29] Humphrey, the tavernkeeper, is called "Misto Tee-
wiley Spillitshops" (335.30–31) —*spille* (Danish) = to play,
act—and "Kitty Cole" is spoken of as "spilling laddy's
measure!" (328.24) ; the man's weapon is likened to a tea-
spoon: "And where was hunty, poppa the gun? Pointing
up to skyless heaven like the spoon out of sergeantmajor's
tay" (330.36–331.2) .[30] Girls, naturally, are "arpists at

cloever spilling" (508.33) ; they "play" (Klaverspil = piano-playing, in Danish) on man's "harp"-strings. Bare-niece Maxwelton has a "hup a' chee" which is "hosch, intra! jist a timblespoon!" (38.16–20) even with her priest. But tea can be "wrongly spilled" (420.33) when the "letter" is miscarried. (Cf. various wrong deliveries cited on p. 420.) When properly used, "Houseanna! Tea is the High-est! For auld lang Ayternitay!" (406.28) . It is the "brew with the foochoor in it" made from a woman-shaped leaf, "a kind of a thinglike all traylogged then pubably it re-symbles a pelvic or some kvind [woman] then props an acutebacked quadrangle with aslant off ohahnthenth a wenchyoumaycuddler, lying with her royalirish uppershoes among the theeckleaves" (608.21–26) . Yet there is more than one indication that "tea" can be spilled in a perverted fashion. The Russian-general story is a "ballet of Gasty Power" that "shocked the rosing girnirilles" and caused a "sad of tearfs" (346.20–21) . And when the teaparty king goes to the "fair" under the assumed names of "Tykingfest [festy-king] and Rabworc [*"elois* Crowbar" or "P. C. Rob-ort" (again, the addition of P and T to the latter name)]" he consorts not only with a girl ("a pedigree pig [*pige*]") but also with a hyacinth (86.7–15). Obviously there is such a thing as erroneous teaspilling.[31] And then, "Kod knows. Anything ruind. Meetingless" (referring to Glugg's sexual failure at his "teapotty": 247.15–16) .[32] So long as woman and her firewater are involved, male fecundity—as symbol-ized by tea—is perpetual and immutable:

> the sameold gamebold adomic structure of our Finnius the old One, as highly charged with electrons as hophazards can effective it, may be there for you, Cockalooralooraloo-menos, when cup, platter and pot come piping hot, as sure as herself pits hen [shits pen] to paper and there's scribings scrawled on eggs [letter (T) written (and sprawled) on X (eggs)]. (615.6–10)

The discussion of tea, however, is not ended by the mere assertion of its fertility symbolism. We must surely see the regenerative connections between tea and the fire-water-whisky which plays such an important part in the *Wake*, and, consequently, between the recuperative powers of these elements and those of the traditional religious symbols, particularly baptism and the wine of the eucharist. If we accept Clive Hart's astute observation that whisky, in *Finnegans Wake*, often stands for the third person of the trinity,[33] the implications continue to multiply. The passage just quoted contains hints of a trinitarian progression: "Finnius the old One" (God), "Cockalooralooraloomenos" (Christ), and the "pot come piping hot" (tea-firewater; the Holy Ghost). Joyce's tea-ology is based on a sexual trinity, an impudent parody of the Christian Father, Son, and Holy Spirit. "A spilt, see [spilled tea, see], for a split, see see [split ecclesiastical authority; is easy]" is the way Juan defines his "chalished drink" (461.35–36). And this pseudo-Christ's extravagant claims for such an outrageous gospel are that it will be at least as well-selling as any other "pious fiction" on the market (440.5–24). That the trinity is sometimes a homosexual one may seem a monstrous proposition, but Joyce's defiant joke does go that far.

8] The

I AM INDEBTED to Bernard Benstock for the extension of the "T" analogies to the word "the" which ends *Finnegans Wake*. Not only does Benstock attach sexual connotations to the word, but he also agrees with other scholars that *Finnegans Wake* is "Joyce's attempt to surpass previous attempts to write 'bibles',"[34] and he argues that HCE steps into the role of the Father-God.

> The various names for Earwicker have their own necessary logic. When H.C.E. is designated as Michael Gunn (as he is here), the significance is that of his role as God the Father: *Makeall Gone* implies the Creator (who made everything) and the Destroyer (who will cause everything to disappear). A glance at some of the other Gunn-God parallels should corroborate this interpretation: *"Duddy Gunne"* (104.8) contains the colloquial form of Father (Daddy), but suggests also "dead and gone" (the crucified Christ, abandoned religion); "gunnfodder" (242.10) is God the Father as well as the sacrificed (canon fodder), an echo of the more literal and ecclesiastical "Canon Futter" (9.19–20); "Gonn the gawds" (257.34) and "Master's gunne" (531.4–5) further serve to indicate Earwicker's position as God, while "Diu! The has goning at gone" (598.9) multiplies the reference with French and Greek (*dieu, theo*). That both *Diu* and *The* have a missing letter suggests the lost phallus of the emasculated god, Osiris, as well as the Christ who disappeared from his tomb and was discovered

to be "gone." The *Wake* significantly ends with the word "the," intended by Joyce to be an aspect of the cyclical pattern, the weak-worded ending rising up again in the continued sentence at the beginning of the book. It is also a modulation from the strongest word in any language, the word for God, to the emasculated form which Joyce considered the weakest word in the English language.[35]

Dublin has always produced swallowers of the gods, according to Joyce, who calls the city "the most phillohippuc [horse-loving] theobibbous [God-drinking (and sacrament-taking)] paùpulation [pope-puling paupers] in the world" (140.12–13). There can be no doubt that *Finnegans Wake* is supposed to be a book about the fall of God, a "book of kills" which dismembers "theos" and records the rise of "the ass." When the ghost of the Father appears to one washerwoman, it is seen by the other as nothing "but a blackburry growth or the dwyergray ass them four old codgers owns" (214.32–33). The ass is "wordless"[36] as compared to the Word-Logos, and yet, somehow, the "dombkey" (dumb key) [37] has a message, even though he is no more than the humble tail-end of the "donkeyman" ("the puisny donkeyman and his crucifer's cauda" [477.22], referring to the ass as a Christopher's cross as well as to the tagging end of a crucified god). Though "dumb," the ass is a "key" to an important secret of the book, for Yawn's revelatory answers from the depths of pre-history are "straight from the ass his mouth" (480.6–7). Such significantly analogical substitutions indicate that Joyce intends to provide blasphemously farcical parodies for the very things that once held him in a near-enchantment of awe and obedience. Several of the names, by which the "untitled mamafesta" has been known at various times, suggest a replacement motif, but the one which refers to the mid-sentence ending of *Finnegans Wake—The Suspended Sentence—*must include a *double entendre*. God may be

guilty,[38] but he is not permanently dead—only petrified—
and Joyce's resurrected "letter" means to reanimate Him
from stone to tree: "Gautamed budders deossiphysing our
Theas" (277.L5).

The analogy of the T-tree phallus to the Holy Trinity
has already been mentioned. *Finnegans Wake* abounds in
further references to the phallus as a substitute for *Theos*.
Yawn's comment that he has found *"la clee* [key] *dang les
champs"* is interpreted by his inquirers as a statement about
"the messiah so cloover" between his legs (478.21–25). And
Finnegan's guest-mourners, gathered at the wake, are said
to be "socializing and communicanting in the deification
of his members" (498.20–21). The central majesty, the fa-
ther-penis, becomes a sugardaddy promising a Nobel prize
to the two sons (thieves) hanging on each side: "Heavy-
sciusgardaddy, parent who offers sweetmeats, will gift uns
his Noblett's surprize. With this laudable purpose in loud
ability let us be singulfied. Betwixt me and thee hung cong.
Item, mizpah ends" (306.3–7). Although the middle figure
is still referred to as "cong" (king), this profane trinity is
hardly regal. The Shem-spirit ("pigeon's pneu") who is to
bear Jaun's letter to Issy is a "kingless" comforter, a substitute for the Jaun-Christ whom Issy feels she can do without very nicely, so long as she has his memory and enough
money (458.26–31). And with the degradation of kingship
comes the debasement of the Father, as symbolized by old
Mark, who is replaced by a jaunty lover, Tristan, the twin
combination which presses the image of sex on the crucifix
form. Should one blame Isolde? "No, no, the dear heaven
knows, and the farther the [Father God] from it, if the
whole stole stale mis betold, whoever the gulpable, and
whatever the pulpous was, the twooned togethered"
(396.21–24).

One has to continue to hold various views, when regarding the three–part male sexual family and the phallic

letter in conjunction with the Holy Trinity and the Christian cross: In one sense, as has already been pointed out, the suggested replacement is a laughable (and pitiable) substitute for the old religious power. "Ty" (T, tea, the) is the tag-end of majesty—"Maggers Tea"—and is certainly no "cruxway . . . to lead us to hopenhaven [hope in either haven or heaven]" (478.15–16). What's left, after scrapping the Father, is the P.S. spoils.[39] In another sense, however, the analogy constitutes the ascription of deity to the most concrete piece of evidence man can offer for the fall and resurrection myth! "Every letter is a godsend," the text assures us, "ardent Ares, brusque Boreas and glib Ganymede like zealous Zeus, the O'Meghisthest of all" (269.17–19). The sexual "the" is still the mightiest and most majestic god of all. The seductress Issy knows this truth, and, with it, how to "betreu" (be true; betray) where her "god" is concerned; "I change thy name though not the letter" (459.31–32), she says, enigmatically, waiting for the return of her "mail."

In certain parts of *Finnegans Wake*, God's fall is spoken of in terms of death. The demise of "the" is included in the description of HCE as "lusting" upon hearing "the cleah whithpeh of a themise" (138.10); and old Chronos is said to be "acrumbling in his sands" while his "sunsunsuns [days; but also Trinitarian progeny] still tumble on" (415.21–22). In other parts, however, God has simply gone away. One version of the letter asks the question: Is God ailing or just flown? "Fool step! Aletheometry [includes both "the" and "om" (the Brahmin mystic equivalent for the name of deity)]?[40] Or just zoot doon floon [Zeus done flown]?" (370.13–14). In any case, He is absent, and His return sometimes seems no more likely than that of the legendary King Arthur. The children, at least, dream their dreams "tell Bappy returns. And Sein annews. We will not say it shall not be, this passing of order and order's

coming, but in the herbest country . . . as in that city self
of legionds they look for its being ever yet" (277.18–22).
Jaun, as the parody of the absent Savior, is confidently expected by his temptress-sister. "Listen, here I'll wait on thee
[the, tea] till Thingavalla with beautiful do be careful tea-
cakes . . . all the time you're awhile way" (460.31–35). However, a strong possibility exists that the Father's holiness,
at least, will soon be forgotten, as Jaun delivers "Theo
Dunnohoo's [don't know whose] warning from Daddy
O'Dowd. Whoo?" (439.19–20). When "the" does return, he
will be "other" than "The" which is gone. "Diu! The has
goning at gone, the is coming to come. Greets to ghastern,
hie to morgning. Dormidy, destady. Doom is the faste. Well
down, good other! ["author," as well as "other"] . . . it is
our hour or risings. Tickle, tickle. Lotus spray. Till here-
next. Adya [Adieu]" (598.9–14). The passage heightens the
hope-despair paradox. The old God is "down"; the new
"the" is greeted as a star of the morning, and yet both
"ghastern" (yesterday) and "morgning" carry deathly connotations in their spellings. The new day is not only the
hour of rising but also the day of doom. And the "Tickle,
tickle" sounds remind us of the ominous handwriting on
the wall in the Biblical story of Nebuchadnezzar's fall:
"Mene, mene, tekel, upharsin" (Daniel 5: 25–28).

Man's break with God is no sudden thing. In fact,
"our Theoatre Regal's drolleries puntomine" (587.7–8) has
been "running strong since creation, *A Royal Divorce*"
(32.32–33) between man and his Maker. Whatever name
he bears, God has always been absent—either dead or else
reigning in some nebulous kingdom—and man has always
promptly killed any earthly incarnations. Butt says, as he
drinks, with wistfulness of absence ("absents wehrmuth"),
to all the past heroes now in Valhalla, "Junglemen in
agleement, I give thee our greatly swooren, Theoccupant
that Rueandredful, the thrownfullvner and all our royal de-

vouts with the arrest of the whole inhibitance of Neui-
lands!" (348.13–16). He is drinking to the memory of the
Russian general, the very father-figure that he claims to
have shot dead.

The resurrection and/or return motif is every bit as
important, in *Finnegans Wake,* as the divorce and death (or
absence) theme. It ought to be plain, however, that what is
being dug up, wet upon, deossified, expected from the sea,[41]
or awakened from the ashes of the Phoenix fire[42] is the
"member" which, according to Joyce, is a good-enough
representation of the modern concept of deity. If religion is
barren, fruitless, lacking the power it once had, the symbol
for such a loss is quite appropriately the lost phallus, which
the Church has damned with the stigma of original sin.[43]
The dead giant, "bewept of his chilidrin and serafim," is
said to be "healed cured and embalsemate, pending a
rouseruction of his bogey, most highly astounded, as it
turned up, after his life overlasting, at thus being reduced
to nothing" (498.33–499.3). Though the King is dead, and
the keening for Him is past, there is still the "key" to be
lifted: "But there's leps of flam in Funnycoon's Wick. The
keyn has passed. Lung lift the keying!" (499.13–14). HCE,
the non-heroic inheritor of all that past majesty, stutters out
his own modest claim to distinction: "I have been reciping
om omominous letters and widely-signed petitions full of
pieces of pottery about my monumentalness as a thinga-
bolls. . . . I considered the lilies on the veldt and unto Balkis
did I disclothe mine glory" (543.6–15). The true second
coming of the God-man may never happen, but the con-
centrated language of the last few lines of *Finnegans Wake*
tells us, in ALP's voice, that, until such a miracle comes
about, her man's "key" will do. "Till thousendsthee. Lps
[Till thou (God, the Father) sends thee (Christ, the son) —
the Second Coming—during that lapse (Lps), he'll pass].

The keys to. Given! [the keys to Heaven—given by lips (Lps) in a kiss]" (628.14–15).

The interpretation just proposed will sound overly sentimental unless one remembers the nearly always comical sense of comedown which accompanies its presentation throughout the book. The little king, compared with the old grand one, is a constant butt for snickering, especially since he is associated with most of the terms one reads on the walls of public lavatories. "Ah, sure, pleasantries aside," says Jaun in his "word apparting," "in the tail of the cow what a humpty daum earth looks our miseryme heretoday as compared beside the Hereweareagain Gaieties of the Afterpiece when the Royal Revolver of these real globoes lets regally fire of his *mio colpo* for the chrisman's pandemon to give over and the Harlequinade to begin properly SPQueaRking Mark Time's Finist Joke. Putting Allspace in a Notshall" (455.23–29). If there *is* a God and a real judgment day, all of this playacting is going to look pretty absurd. Joyce sees himself as the Shem-shape of the creator, and at the same time mocks himself as a perversion of deity. It is of note that one method of "killing" the Father, as evidenced in the Captain and tailor and the Russian general stories (as well as in the park episode), is homosexual union—man replacing God by uniting with Him pervertedly. And part of the destruction of *Theos* is accomplished by the destructive parody of Joyce as the God-like author. Shem's treatment is devastating; he comes under murderous—but comic—attack, and is constantly alluded to as a low, invert-type. If he is one aspect of the new godhead —as I believe he is—he brings to it some shocking qualities; "people said [of Shem-Glugg] he'd shape of hegoat where he just was sheep of herrgott with his tile togged. Top" (240.34–35).[44] The depiction of Shem, in each of his roles, is unquestionably a self-caricature on Joyce's part. Never-

theless, the "hand of Sameas" (483.4) prevails in the end—
in creative control. Shem, "sacrificed," rises again; the new
word-world is *Finnegans Wake,* which ends with the small-
god word, "the." The "revolution of the Word" is Joyce's
revolution of the world.

One can recall Buck Mulligan's insistence that
Shephen Dedalus, with his "absurd" Greek name, ought to
work for a "new paganism," Hellenizing the Irish. Joyce,
moving away from the impotent Stephen, has finally an-
thropomorphized the gods in *Finnegans Wake.* Perhaps,
like Osiris' son Horus, he does it for vengeance, castrating
the Stephen-Set murderer of the Father-God, and, as the
son born of a reconstructed sexual deity, starting a whole
new generation of human gods. For the letter dug out of
the muck salvages a trinity which looks very much like
man himself, who, though he is bound to carry forever the
hump-like burden of guilt for his misbehavings, is used
to "summits" and falls, and is "not so giddy any more"
(624.11–12) . "Every letter is a hard," says ALP to HCE,
"but yours sure is the hardest crux ever. Hack an axe, hook
an oxe, hath an an, heth hith ences [sins; mistakes]. But
once done, dealt and delivered, tattat, you're on the map.
Rased on traumscrapt from Maston, Boss. After rounding
his world of ancient days" (623.33–624.1) .

3

KEY FIGURES

9] *Three, Two, and One*

IN THE VERY first chapter of *Finnegans Wake,* Mutt shows Jute the significant landmarks and the relics which symbolize and recall the history of man. The past can be turned up as re-plowed earth ("furrowards, bagawards"), and the under-side may be read as a "claybook." " (Stoop) if you are abcedminded, to this claybook, what curios of signs (please stoop), in this allaphbed! Can you rede . . . its world? It is the same told of all. Many. Miscegenations on miscegenations. Tieckle. They lived und laughed ant loved end left. Forsin. Thy thingdome is given to the Meades and Porsons" (18.17–22) .[1] Small relics stand for larger things ("Futhorc, this liffle effingee [effigy; FNG ("fing" or "thing")] is for a firefing called a flintforfall [a gun causing a fall]": 18.34–35) . But larger things may also stand for small parts, and, here, Joyce announces his technique of constantly turning synecdoche, inverted over and over: "When a part so ptee [petit (but also P and T)] does duty for the holos [whole; hole] we soon grow to use of an

allforabit [the whole for the part]" (18.36–19.2) . "Allforabit," of course, provides another metaphor which is useful
in understanding the author's method. The use of "letters"
as symbols—P and T, for instance ("ptee") —establishes the
need for an alphabet, a large body of symbols which stands
for language. The same system works when you begin with
sexual parts and eventually decide to make larger "things"
act for the "language" such sexual "letters" represent. So
HCE is created to "stand for" his own sexual parts, and ALP
comes to life as the synecdoche for woman's sexual parts.
Joyce goes further: numbers, too, are made to be symbols
parallel to letters. Three stands for T; two stands for P;
three soldiers are "whole" people who represent the man's
tripartite privates, and two "jinnies" are the woman's bi-
labial genitals (*"Privates Earwicker and a Pair of Sloppy
Sluts"*: 107.6) . One clue for the name of Finn MacCool in
the quiz chapter (I, vi) is "a part of the whole as a port for
a whale" (135.28–29) , and even HCE's inn, somehow, becomes not only a part for the whole ("leporty hole") but
also a malt T (ea)house symbolizing a T-hole in a door—
"amaltheouse for leporty hole" (338.20) . The device serves,
by turns, to universalize the particular, and to concretize
the universally abstract. It is one way Joyce manages to deal
with many levels at one time.

Clive Hart's *Concordance*[2] lists 161 direct uses of the
number three and 275 uses of the number two,[3] plus many
more linguistic variations of those numbers, including compound Latinate words using forms of the prefixes tri- and
duo-, and also forms from other languages. The count is
impressive when compared to that of the other numbers
from one to ten. (The relationships among three, T, tea,
tree, and "the" would provide many more listings in the
sections entitled "Syllabifications" and "Overtones" in
Hart's volume.) When the number three appears in some
form, the number two (or a variant of it) may be found in

close proximity approximately fifty percent of the time. That three and two are the sexual numbers, respectively, for the man and the woman is borne out by numerous unmistakable references: "The threelegged man and the tulippied dewydress" (331.8–9); "leandros three bumped heroines two [Leander's three bumped Hero's two]" (203.13–14); "three tommix, soldiers free, cockaleak and cappapee" (58.24–25); "It's good for her bilabials, you understand" (465.26); "twalegged poneys [jinnies] and threehandled dorkeys [door keys; darkeys; donkeys]" (285.13–14); "The dirty dubs upin [open] their flies, went too free [one, two, three], echoed the dainly drabs downin their scenities [scented panties; obscenities], una mona [one, one]" (60.35–61.1).

The three and the two are to be thought of as single units—three-in-one man, two-in-one woman—but also as a family of five: the father flanked by two sons on the male side, and the wife and daughter on the female. "I," says HCE, "be the forced generation of group marriage . . . I, huddled til summone be the massproduct of teamwork, three surtouts wripped up in itchother's, two twin pritti- coaxes lived as one, troubled in trine or dubildin too . . . most surely I pretend and reclam to opt for simultaneous" (546.12–23). And Issy confirms her twin-type union with her mother: "but me and meother [my other; mother] ravin, my coosine of mine, have mour good three chancers, weothers, after Bohnaparts. The mything smile of me, my wholesole assumption, shes nowt mewithout as weam twin herewithin, that I love like myselfish. . . . How their duel makes their triel!" (238.25–31). The two brothers continually refer to the third "person" which stands between them (e.g., 526.11–15; 465.17–18; 360.3–5), and there is ample evidence that the sinned against and the sinner (s) are the same—that only the one sexual family is involved. The composite and/or multiple identities of the family, as the roles of the members shift, are forever fluid. The two may be Issy and her make-believe looking-glass companion; Anna and Isabel; ALP's or Isolde's genitals; the two girls in the park who stand for the female aspect of HCE's fornication; the two jinnies involved in the "Willingdone" episode, who fight a urinating battle with the "lipoleums." The three are alternately (sometimes simultaneously) the father, in any of his roles, accompanied by the sons, in any of their roles; the father's genitals; the three soldiers in the park who stand for the agents involved in the homesexual encounter; the three lipoleums; and all the variations of T discussed earlier. Any single explanation of the numerous relationships is bound to be muddling: "It is a mere mienerism of this vague of visibilities," explains the narrator, in a baffling fashion,

> as in pure . . . essenesse [essence; S and S (Shem and Shaun) ; SNS (N for "Nobodaddy"?)], there have been disselving forenenst you just the draeper [the tailor; Swift], the two drawpers assisters [drawers (of the) sisters; draper's assistants] and the three droopers assessors confraternitisers. Who are, of course, Uncle Arth, your [arse; Arthur] two cozes from Niece and . . . our own familiars, Billyhealy, Ballyhooly and Bullyhowley, surprised in an indecorous position by the Sigurd Sigerson Sphygmomanometer [sphincter; Sphinx; mom and home; om-man-om; etcetera] Society for bledprusshers [blood pressure (since sphygmomanometer is an instrument for measuring arterial blood pressure) ; bed pressers; bloody prussians]. (608.1–11)

How is one to make sense out of the entanglements?

First, one must remember the fact, confirmed by nearly all *Wake* scholars, that, for Joyce, there are two or more sides to everything, and must accept, further, the virtual certainty that everything will include a sexual side. Since the sexual symbolism is, as I believe, central to the meaning of the entire book, no one should be surprised that the copulative manifestation of dualistic opposition involves both hetero- and homesexuality (plus many other sexual aberrations). The witness called forth from Yawn's unconscious makes an impassioned rationalization for the defendant's "bisectualism": "Supposing . . . him . . . to have taken his epscene licence before the norsect's divisional respectively as regards them male privates and or concomitantly with all common or neuter respects to them public exess [pubic X's] females," he argues, and goes on to defend "the merits of early bisectualism," citing metaphorical examples of a "cunifarm school of herring [Herr; her; erring; aryan; Arian heresy]." And "them little up-andown dippies they was all of a libidous pickpuckparty and raid on a wriggolo finsky [on a regular fence; a wriggling Finn] doodah in testimonials to their early bisectualism. Such," says the witness, "is how the reverend Coppinger, he visualises the hidebound homelies of creed crux ethics." "Tallhell and Barbados wi ye and your Errian coprulation!" exclaims the questioner. "Y'are absexed, so y'are, with mackerglosia and mickroocyphyllicks" (523.33–525.9). "Mackerglosia," combining the prefix "macro" with "gloss" (misleading interpretation) and with "glossitis" (inflamation of the tongue) is paralled to "mickroocyphyllicks," combining "micro" with "cipher" (secret method of writing) and with syphillis ("inflamation" at the other end); the comparison provides additional suggestion of tabooed subjects and perversion. The two "faces" to all questions are, on the one hand, symbolized by mouth and either vagina or anus: faces oppose feces; eating opposes defecating or copulating; firewater is drunk and firewater is spilled (tea: semen or urine). But entry and exit must also be viewed as front and rear—and, in *Finnegans Wake*, the many instances of entrance through the back door call special attention to a two-valued emphasis.[4]

Included in the names of the *Wake* letter is the title, *"Divine Views from Back to the Front"* (106.28) . And the price for the visit to "Madam's Toshowus's" wax museum ("entrance, one kudos [*dos* = two]; exits, free [three]: 57.20–21) establishes the connection linking two to the front and three to the rear. One of the sins of the defendant at the trial must have been of a backdoor variety, for one witness, accepting heterosexuality, says that you can't blame man for his misdemeanors with girls, "but I also think, Puellywally, by the *siege* of his trousers there was someone else *behind* it—you bet your *boughtem* blarneys—about their *three* drummers down *Keysars* Lane. (*Trite!*) " (61.24–27; italics mine) . "Gricks may rise and Troysirs fall (there being two sights for ever a picture) ," says the guide of the Museyroom. "Let young wimman run away with the story and let young min talk smooth behind the butteler's back. . . . So true is it that therewhere's a turnover the tay is wet too and when you think you ketch sight of a hind make sure but you're cocked by a hin" (11.35–12.17). While the *Wake* hero may have every normal inclination toward what is ahead and what is inevitable for human survival, he must always be cursed by an opposite tendency to look back at his original sins. And thus Finn MacCool is characterized in the quiz chapter: "though his heart, soul and spirit turn to pharaoph times, his love, faith and hope stick to futuerism; light leglifters cense him souriantes from afore while boor browbenders curse him grommelants to his hindmost; between youlasses and yeladst glimpse of Even" (129.35–130.3) . For he "sas [sows] seed enough for a semination but sues skivvies on the sly" (130.17–18) . HCE, too, thoughtfully reviewing the captain and the tailor story, stutters out a confession of identification with such "queer" tendencies.

It is that something, awe, aurorbean [coming up like the dawn (aurorean) or aurora borealis] in that fellow, hamid

and damid . . . which comequeers this anywhat perssian which we, owe, realisinus [realize in us] with purups a dard of pene [we see ourselves guiltily, as having queer tendencies]. There is among others pleasons [persons; pleasing sons] whom I love and which are favourests to mind, one which I have pushed my finker in for the movement and . . . she [ambiguous sex] is highly catatheristic [cathartic (purgative); catatonic (describing a syndrome of schizophrenia—hence, representative of alternation, doublesexed)] and there is another which I have fombly fongered freequuntly [front; female genitals] and . . . she is deeply sangnificant [significant; sanguiforous (conveying blood)].
(357.6–15)

HCE calls these varied activities "alternate nightjoys" (line 18), suggesting a relaxation of taboo in dreams but also indicating his all-inclusiveness as "man." Someone will always bring charges against the person committing either of these "offenses." Women charge "rape," while men dog the pervert offender with blackmail. "If violence to life, limb and chattels, often as not, has been the expression, direct or through an agent male, of womanhid offended, (ah! ah!), has not levy of black mail [blackmail; back male] from the times the fairies were in it, and fain for wilde erthe blothoms followed an impressive private reputation for whispered sins?" (68.36–69.4; the allusion is to Oscar Wilde's "whispered sins."[5]).

Joyce is not simply indulging his urge to include in *Finnegans Wake* every tabooed subject he can think of; for purposes of a tight symbolic pattern, he seems to stress the expression of male-to-male intercourse in sodomy (that is, anal homosexuality between two male humans). One must somehow visualize a two-sided protagonist, acting heterosexually in one direction and allowing himself to be acted upon, homosexually, behind his back. There is an indication that, if the three "privates" made their advances to the front (to the "three" of the male), their "suits"—like the first two suits of the perverted tailor (s) —would be rejected[6]: too many "threes." "Nobody will know or heed you, *Post*umus, if you skip round schlymartin by the *back* and come *front* sloomutren to beg in [beg for; begin] one of the shavers' sailor*suits*. Three climbs threequickenthrees in the garb of nine" (377.9–12; italics mine) . The forward confrontation must involve the "three" and the "two", whereas, in the rear encounter, the "three" acts upon the "one": "cumbrum, cumbrum, twiniceynurseys fore a drum but tre to uno tips the scale" (134.8–9) ; or, to put it in more ambiguous language, "Ena milo melomon, frai is frau and swee is too, swee is two when swoo is free, ana mala woe is we! A pair of sycopanties with amygdaleine eyes, one old obster lumpky pumpkin and three meddlars on their slies" (94.14–18) .[7]

The two-sided theme of the three, the two, and the one is used primarily in the accounts of the incidents in the park. Whether the meeting with the three happened before or after the meeting with the two is apparently not important. Nor does it matter that the events are sometimes spoken of as merely micturating and/or defecating incidents. Indeed, HCE claims they were only a case of exposure both ways; he has been misunderstood. "Guilty but fellows culpows [fellow culprits; felix culpa]!" He only

> spake to approach from inherdoff trisspass through minxmingled hair. Though I may have hawked it, said, and selled my how hot peas after theactrisscalls from my imprecurious position and though achance I could have emptied a pan of backslop down drain by whiles of dodging a rere from the middenprivet appurtenant thereof . . . I am ever incalpable [incapable; non-culpable] . . . of unlifting upfallen girls wherein dangered from them in thereopen out of unaduleratous bowery, with those hintering influences from an angelsexonism. It was merely my barely till their oh offs. Missaunderstaid. (363.20–36)

Later, however, in the same speech, he changes his protest to a statement that he merely "felt" the little girls.

> My little love apprencisses, my dears, the estelles, van Nessies von Nixies voon der pool, which I had a reyal devouts for yet was it marly lowease or just a feel with these. . . . A nexistence of vividence! . . . if that is grace for the grass what is balm for the bramblers . . . that I am the catasthmatic old ruffin sippahsedly improctor to be seducint trovatellas, the dire daffy damedeaconesses, like . . . the lilliths oft I feldt . . . then . . . I'll tall tale tell croon paysecurers . . . that thash on me stumpen blows the gaff off mombition and thit thides or marse [the ides of March; the hides of me arse] makes a good dayle to be shattat. Fall stuff.

The longer he speaks, the more he implicates himself. His excuse for sodomy, finally, is that he thrust his hole sort of close when the other fellow's "rod," half stiff, was in the air. ("His rote in ere, afstef, was. And dong wonged Magongty till the bombtomb of the warr, thrusshed in his whole soort of cloose.") [8] In another context, both sins are blamed on someone else, a person who resembles the defendant, named "Deucollion" (cf. the Deucalion and Pyrrha myth, where stones become men; also, M.E. "coillons" = testicles).

> The tew cherripickers, with their Catheringnettes, Lizzy and Lissy Mycock . . . were they moon at aube [dawn] with hespermun [Hesperian (evening); sperm] and I their covin guardient [secret ingredient; cover guard], I would not know to contact such gretched youngsteys in my ways from Haddem [I would not know them from Adam] or any suitstersees or heiresses of theirn. . . . Her [here] is one which rassembled to mein enormally. . . . He is Deucollion. Each habe goheerd, uptaking you are inersence, but we sen you meet sose infance. Deucollion! [We seen you meet those infants, Deucollion].

But, it is objected, you (HCE) were the one who "hard casted thereass pigstenes upann Congan's shootsmen in Schottenhof, ekeascent [not so?]? Igen [again]," says HCE, "Deucollion!" But he gives himself away in *double entendre*: "I liked his Gothamm chic [cheek]!" (538.21-33) . What happened in the park is finally inseparable from the double-sexed symbolism, and Joyce makes it clear that the homosexual "bottom"—though its "depression" is a Hell-hole as well as Valhalla—is not, by any means, to be ignored (564.34-565.2) . The two episodes are most lucidly described in that most un-lucid chapter which tells the stories of the perversions of the captain and of the Russian general.

> Imagine twee cweamy wosen. Suppwose you get a beautiful thought and cull them sylvias sub silence. Then inmaggin a stotterer. Suppoutre him to been one biggermaster Omnibil. Then lustily (tutu the font and tritt on the bokswoods like gay feeters's dance) immengine up to three longly lurking lobstarts. . . . Pet her, pink him, play pranks with them. She will nod amproperly smile. He may seem to appraisiate it. They are as piractical jukersmen sure to paltipsypote [participate]. . . . How do, dainty daulimbs? . . . Heyday too, Malster Faunagon, and hopes your hahititahiti licks the mankey nuts! And oodlum hoodlum doodlum to yes, Donn, Teague and Hurleg, who the bullocks brought you here and how the hillocks are ye? (337.16-31) [9]

The idea of battle, as associated with the pre-marital meetings of the two, the three, and the one, is brought out in the variation on the park encounters in which the protagonists are "Willingdone," the three "lipoleums," and the two "jinnies." Kate tells the story as she recalls it upon reviewing the relics in the "museyroom": the "Crossgun," the "triplewon hat," the "big wide harse." The Jinnies shower "irrigating" dispatches on Willingdone; the dispatches hit "me Belchum," the Welsh lipoleum between the two "bag" and "bug" lipoleums,[10] and defecating dispatches are hurled back. The two "sides" are fighting, and Willingdone is in the center of it all.

> This is his big wide harse. Tip. This is the three lipoleum boyne grouching down in the living detch. This is an inimyskilling inglis, this is a scotcher grey, this is a davy, stooping. This is the bog lipoleum mordering the lipoleum beg. . . . This is the petty lipoleum boy that was nayther bag nor bug. . . . This is Delian alps. This is Mont Tivel, this is Mont Tipsey, this is the Grand Mons Injun. This is the crimealine of the alps hooping to sheltershock the three lipoleums.[11] This is the jinnies with their legahorns feinting to read in their handmade's book of stralegy while making their war undisides the Willingdone. The jinnies is a cooin her hand and the jinnies is a ravin her hair and the Willingdone git the band up. This is big Willingdone mormorial tallowscoop Wounderworker obscides on the flanks of the jinnies. Sexcaliber hrosspower. Tip. This is me Belchum sneaking his phillippy out of his most Awful Grimmest Sunshat Cromwelly. Looted. This is the jinnies' hastings dispatch for to irrigate the Willingdone. Dispatch in thin red lines cross the shortfront of me Belchum. . . . That was the tictacs of the jinnies for to fontannoy the Willingdone. Shee, shee, shee! The jinnies is jillous agincourting all the lipoleums. And the lipoleums is gonn boycottoncrezy onto the one Willingdone. And the Willingdone git the band up. This is bode Belchum, bonnet to busby, breaking his secred word with a ball up his ear to the Willingdone. This is the Willingdone's hurold dispitchback. Dispitch desployed on the regions rare [rear] of me Belchum. . . . That was the first joke of Willingdone, tic for tac. (8.21–9.15)

Anyone knows that "three upon one is by inspection improper" (131.32–33). Upon the marriage of the captain to the tailor's daughter, the "ships gospfather" advises that there be "no more of your maimed acts after this with your kowtoros and criados to every tome, thick and heavy, and our onliness of his revelance to your ultitude" (325.33–35). (Joyce is also commanding, here, that attention be detracted, from now on, from the Bible and other tomes, thick and heavy.) And the commandment from the four, after witnessing the Butt and Taff reenactment of the Russian general episode, is "to let the gentlemen pedestarolies . . . live his own left leave. . . . And not to not be always . . . treeing unselves up with one exite . . . about the back excits" (368.11–19). Even on the Tunc page, the commentator sees evidence of perversion as the dark, tabooed sin: "there are exactly three squads of candidates for the crucian rose [all male] awaiting their turn in the marginal panels of Columkiller, chugged in their three ballotboxes . . . where two was enough for anyone . . . since then people speaking have fallen into the custom . . . of saying two is company when the third person is the person darkly spoken of" (122.24–31). Nevertheless, the encounter with the "two," when it is mentioned in connection with the three-and-one mating, is every bit as sinful to the gossipers who tell and retell the double-event: "they found him guilty of . . . those imputations of fornicolopulation with two of his albowcrural correlations on whom he was said to have enjoyed by anticipation when schooling them in amown, mid grass . . . but . . . of some deretane denudation with intent to excitation, caused by his retrogradation, among firearmed forces [the three privates]" (557.16–23). Obviously, the three-and-two and three-and-one episodes are each pre-civilized transgressions. Both the two-sided, fluctuating male and the fornicating female are admonished to renounce these dry, ossifying activities and to get married. "Posidonius O'Fluctuary! Lave that bloody stone as it is! What are you doing your dirty minx and his big treeblock way up your path? Slip around, you, by the rare of the ministers'!" (80.28–31). The mother-hen figure steps in to rescue the erring male, for "she feel plain plate one flat fact thing and if, lastways firdstwise, a man alones sine anyon anyons utharas has no rates to done a kik at with anyon anakars about tutus milking fores and the rereres on the outerrand asikin the tutus to be forrarder" (113.5–9). So there is actually a tri-partite progression in the fundamental sexual events of the male life-cycle: "once was he shovelled [*cheval*—thus "horsed" (by the jinnies)] and once was he arsoned [fired up by sodomy] and once was he inundered [buried] and she hung him out billbailey" (127.4–6). The implication is that the first two acts lead to "death." And so there is a connection between "stone" and these back-door events. As usual, tree and stone correspond with front and rear.[12] But they also stand for life and death: "Their livetree (may it flourish!) by their ecotaph (let it stayne!)" (420.11–12). There is a "dud letter" (129.7) of the past that requires banal Anna to bang it into shape.

The idea that the two acts of fornication are separate from the third act of fruitful mating is borne out by the consistent treatment of those sins as belonging to the vague, partly remembered past. (Cf. 135.11–13). ALP, as the mother-figure, finally establishes a home, which is to be sharply distinguished from a hotel or a brothel: "Every ditcher's dastard in Dupling will let us know about it," warns the observer of the copulation of old "Humperfeldt and Anunska," "if you have paid the mulctman by whether your rent is open to be foreclosed or aback in your arrears. This is seriously meant. Here is a homelet not a hothel" (586.15–18). The hen's rescue of the letter unearths fresh records of those past events, it is true, but also makes possible their incorporation and acceptance into a new whole man. The "marriage," too, is a two-to-three affair, and involves a battle, like the one between the Prankquean and the Earl of Howth, or like the battles at the Wake, where " 'Twas womans' too [two]woman with mans' throw [three] man" (511.23). So the "three-times-is-a-charm" motif of the stories already discussed—the Prankquean, the captain and the tailor, and the Russian general—becomes a thematic indication of Joyce's view of the life cycle and also of the total structure of the book. The three will become one in the father, and though "Nircississies are as the doaters of inversion," "Secilas [Alices] through their laughing classes [looking glasses] [will become] poolermates in laker life" (526.34–36).

10] *Plain Geometry*

THE "universe" of *Finnegans Wake* is already shaping up by letter and by number, and it appears that Joyce also wanted to give it some geometrical form. The problems are vexatious, for, as Hart has observed, "Literally dozens of formal patterns are superimposed upon one another and closely interwoven in the texture."[13] The artist-creator has given us one sexual diagram as a start; if we begin with this two-dimensional figure and work up to three, four, and even more dimensions, I believe it may be possible to get at least an imaginary glimpse of the model Joyce had in his amazing mind.

In the "Night Lessons" chapter (II, ii), we are told that Kev is very poor at figures, has had to learn to count on his fingers (282.7–17), and has always "caught allmeals dullmarks for his nucleuds and alegobrew" (283.23–24). One of the problems that gives him trouble is this: "Show that the median, hce che ech, interecting at royde angles the parilegs of a given obtuse one biscuts both the arcs that are in curveachord behind. Brickbaths. The family umbroglia" (283.36–284.4). The median—a line through the vertex of a triangle, bisecting the opposite side—is obviously the triple-T (hce, che ech) of the male entering (intererecting, intersecting, interacting) the female triangle at its point and bisecting the "arcs" of the "behind," behind brick paths. The bisector is called the family umbrella, but

to Kev it is "imbroglio," a confusing state of affairs. It
will be recognized that this problem is nearly the same as
the one Dolph will explain to his brother later on in the
chapter (the diagram for which is reproduced on FW 293),
except that it includes not only the arcs and the triangle
but the bisector as well. It seems extremely simple.

The next problem raised, however, is far more complex, and is an indication that we cannot depend on two-
dimensional diagrams for full understanding.

> A Tullagrove pole [a three-dimensional HCE] to the
> Height of County Fearmanagh has a septain [certain;
> septum (dividing wall or membrane in a plant or animal)]
> inclinaison [inclination; liaison] and the graphplot[14] for
> all the functions in Lower County Monachan, whereat
> samething is rivisible [reversible; divisible; revisible] by
> nighttim, may be involted into the zeroic couplet, palls pell
> inhis heventh glike noughty times ∞ [symbol for infinity],
> find, if you are not literally cooefficient, how minney
> combinaisies and permutandies can be played on the inter-
> national surd! pthwndxrclzp!,[15] hids cubid rute being ex-
> tructed, taking anan illitterettes, ififif at a tom. Answers,
> (for teasers [teachers] only). Ten, twent, thirt, see, ex and
> three icky totchty ones [C (100), X (10) and three ones
> (111)] (284.5–17)

When a third dimension plus infinity is introduced, and
when the "dividends" are multiplied ("anan illitterettes,
ififif at a tom"), one begins to let lost in the combinations
and permutations that result. The next problem is so all-
inclusive ("Imagine the twelve deaferended dumbbawls
of the whowl abovebeugled to be the contonuation through
regeneration of the urutteration of the word in pregross"
[284.18–22]) that it even includes the seasons and the longi-
tudinal and latitudinal directions, and when *that* composite
is reversed, by a Merlin-magical turning of the table, the
solution is practically impossible, for the result is "Equal
to=aosch" (chaos: 286.2).[16]

But "P.t.l.o.a.t.o" (please to lick one and turn over);
get on the right side of the "table" for a problem that can
be solved. We are to start with an easy figure which even
Kevin ought to be able to understand. "Concoct an equo-
angular trillitter" (286.21–22). The word "trillitter" suggests not only ALP's triangle but also the tri-letter T and
the "litter" consisting of the three children. The figure to
be imagined is a triangle bisected not by just a T, but by
an E. (In each of these problems, the bisecting represents
the sexual act.) With the base of the triangle, the E forms
a square and the composite becomes the Aristotelian symbol for unified body and soul—the square imposed on the
triangle[17]—altered by its being *bisected*. *(See Figure 1.)*
This basic two-dimensional pattern includes the five geo-

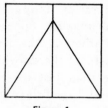

Figure 1

metric symbols Joyce used for his Earwicker family
(E ⊏ △ ∧ ⊣), plus the square which signifies the title of
the book.[18] Bisexualism must immediately be apprehended
in such a diagram, for Issy is a T, although her "crossing"
(the door) is the base of the triangle, and the two triangles
she forms are right-angled duplicates (the daughter and
her mirror image). Shaun, as ∧, is part of a female triangle—
minus the "door," while Shem, ⊏, lacks his father's penis.[19]

The figure that Dolph actually draws for Kev, however, does not show the bisectors T and E. It is, on the
simplest level, a picture of the mother sitting "cresslogged-
like the lass that lured a tailor" (297.28–29). Dolph care-
fully instructs his brother, line by line, in the construction

of the diagram. The result is a figurative drawing of "the whome [womb; whom; home; hole] of your eternal geomater" (296.31–297.1). The lower part no doubt resembles ALP, "Mother of us all" (299.3) —her triangular pudenda and the arcs of her lower extremities. But Kev does not at first see the triangle that is, appropriately, below the water line.[20] He has to be guided by lamp to the "bluishing refluction" in the water below. The "real" representation of the mother ALP is the triangle above, and the lower triangle appears to be a dark, shadowy reminder of Eve 's fall. (See "Dawn gives rise. . . . Eve takes fall": 293.30–31.) It is a figure of another mysterious mirror-world, where directions and spatial measurements are unreliable. Dolph's language supports this impression. "I remumble," he says, "from the yules gone by, purr lil murrerof myhind [mother of mankind; mirror of my (be) hind]" (295.4–6).[21] So, whereas it is true that the upper point, π, represents Anna Livia's navel ("where . . . its naval's napex will have to beandbe" [297.12–14]), the drawing apparently is supposed to show more than just the lower extremies of a woman. If the diamond-shaped rhombus, as a whole, is "the no niggard spot of her safety vulve" (297.26–27), it is as well, in its two parts, the double-nature of the woman: mother and temptress, "poolermates in laker life" (526.36).

But the diagram's double nature applies not only to the woman. The interchange between Dolph and Kev in this section makes it plain that both of the twins are represented by the drawing. In the first place, the two circles are the twin "pair of accomplasses"[22] working on the problem. They are distinguished by Kev: "You [Dolph], allus for the kunst [art] and me for omething with a handel to it [sacred (om) music (Handel); also "Handel" (German) = trade, commerce]" (295.27–29). The differentiation also refers to the sexual preferences of each of the twins, again bringing up the double-sexed theme and indicating that Kev (the Shaun twin) is probably the "female" partner in any homosexual symbolism.

> "Now . . . there's tew tricklesome poinds where our twain of doubling bicirculars, mating approxemetely in their suite poi and poi, dunloop into eath the ocher. Lucihere.!" "I fee where you mea. The doubleviewed seeds." . . . "I'd likelong, by Araxes, to mack a capital Pee for Pride down there on the batom where Hoddum and Heave, our mon-sterbilker, balked his bawd of parodies. And let you go, Airmienious, and mick your modest mock Pie out of Humbles up your end. Where your apexojesus [apex; exegesis; Christ-likeness] will be a point of order. . . . Are you right there, Michael, are you right? Do you think you can hold on by sitting tight?" "Well, of course, it's awful angelous. Still I don't feel it's so dangelous. Ay, I'm right here, Nickel, and I'll write. Singing the top line why it suits me mikey fine."[23]   (295.29–296.19)

The apex of what comes to be the upper triangle is the point of "order" assigned to Kev as the heavenly Mick (the militant archangel, Michael), whereas the lower vertex is designated as belonging to Dolph, the devilish Nick. The bottom ("batom") point is associated with Lucifer and the pride which not only caused his own fall but also meant the loss of paradise ("parodies") [24] for Adam and Eve (who are significantly treated as *one male* masterbuilder, Finnegan, the hod-carrier). At the top, "Mick" sits eating mock-humble pie ("Humbles" = humbug; π), singing his hymns like an airminded Arminius (a Dutch heretic theologian, advocate of free will). So the triangles and the circles have meaning as figures representing the twins as well as both ALP and her temptress-daughter.

That is not all, however, not by any means. The "mating" of the circles suggests at least temporary unification of the twins—in male-to-male sexual activity but also in a coming-together as one figure. "I fee where you mea" can be translated two ways: "I see what you mean," and "I feel where you are me." Such a union should alert us to the presence of the father, the third member of a trinity that becomes whole only by his appearance. Yes, the master-builder-swindler ("monsterbilker") is here, too. The drawing is bisexual, and if we can imagine the "beckside" of the figure, we will see that HCE can be depicted in circles as well as in right-angled lines (Cf. 58.3–4). "Finn his park" is elsewhere described as our father-male's rear.

> Is it not that we are commanding from fullback, woman permitting, a profusely fine birdseye view from beauhind this park? . . . The straight road down the center [here, the "bisector" is included in the image] (see relief map) bisexes the park which is said to be the largest of his kind in the world. On the right prominence confronts you the handsome vinesregent's lodge while, turning to the other supreme piece of cheeks, exactly opposite, you are confounded by the equally handsome chief sacristary's residence. Around is a little amiably tufted and man is cheered when he bewonders through the boskage how the nature in all frisko is enlivened by gentlemen's seats. (564.6–17)

After all, "the effrays" in this book are all "round father-thyme's beckside" (90.7). And what has "thyme" to do with this two-dimensional figure?

In the account of creation in Plato's *Timaeus*,[25] the circles of the "Same" and the "Other" are set in counter-revolution—one inside the other—as dual parts of the World Soul.[26] The corresponding image in *Finnegans Wake* is a three-dimensional figure in which, as Joyce evidently pictured it, Shaun moves in a clockwise, East-West direction (the exterior circle of the Same), and Shem moves in a counter-clockwise, North-South direction (the interior—and inferior—circle of the Other). If we, figuratively, pull the circles out of orbit and flatten them out to two dimensions, with the arcs overlapping at the center, we have an approximation of the figure-eight symbol for infinity. As Hart says, "when Joyce has cut the circles and stretched them out flat, the other nodal point falls exactly in the centre of the fabric. Represented in this way, the basic structure of *Finnegans Wake* thus looks rather like a figure 8 on its side, which forms the 'zeroic couplet' (284.11) ∞, or the symbol for 'infinity'."[27] But Joyce wants to combine his "perfect bodies" in one "stable somebody"; he distorts the figure eight so that it will enclose the two triangles which, if linked with each other, would form a Solomon's seal, the six-pointed star representing, in ancient symbolism, infinity of space multiplied by infinity of time.[28] "And if you flung her headdress on her from under her highlows you'd wheeze whyse Salmonson set his seel on a hexengown" (297.1–4). (*See Figure 2.*) Shem's drawing is said to have "sixuous parts" (297.22), and Issy's note (297,n.1) calls this esoteric

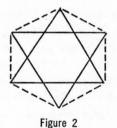

Figure 2

shape the hope of the nation ("The chape of Doña Speranza of the Nacion"). Joyce, offering us graphically and insistently his "geomater," who is, after all, the eternal bride of God, emphasizes the identification of time with woman, the river, the constant flow. There is no history without sex, since history—time—is the female force. Universal space has no meaning or shape without that dimension.

The possibilities of the all-inclusive diagram are far from being exhausted. One can begin to understand the way in which Joyce was able to integrate all of his structural patterns symbolically, by superimposing the E, in its proper "bisecting" position, upon the basic two-dimensional structure Dolph has drawn for Kev. (*See Figure 3.*) The result

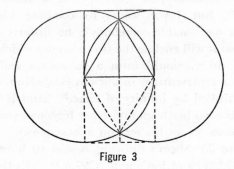

Figure 3

is a completion of the "trillitter" mentioned on 286.22, a unification of Everyman's and Everywoman's Body with World Soul, and of infinite time with infinite space. Another reason for Joyce's playing with geometric symbols can immediately be seen: the historical and mystical implications made possible through the reconciliation of ancient magical symbolism and modern science. To see "how minney combinaisies and permutandies can be played on the international surd," we need only to start extending lines from these basic shapes in all directions. The lines of the triangles will form spokes of wheels, larger triangles, hexagons; those of the T will divide as many equilaterals as we like into right-angled Issy-triangles with mirror images;[29] the E, up-ended and moved from side to side, will form quincunxes, and squares and squares of bisectors in both proper and perverse positions;[30] circles will compose bicycles and tricycles, mandalas, and flowers all over the place. Such an expanding method of design illustrates very effectively Joyce's method of elaboration and decoration of the "word," and it also emphasizes Joyce's formal means of making certain that his ordinary little family, interacting with one another, will be recognized as representative of every possible aspect of human existence.

Nevertheless, the two-dimensional explanation is for beginners, like Kev. Nothing is static in *Finnegans Wake*; its constant flux can be likened most effectively, I think, to the phenomenon of expansion and contraction in molecular activity when matter changes state. The device of synecdoche has already demonstrated the tendency of certain aggregates to stand for objects both minute and immense, and, in this particular geometry lesson, Dolph reflects that "we're only all telescopes. Or the comeallyoum saunds" (295.11–12), directing our attention to the fact that each of these "persons" is liable to be seen at any given moments as small as a grain of sand or as enormous as the universe—increasing and decreasing in either spatial or sound volume according to the point of observation determined by a whimsical creator, and according to whether we are to be interpreting the novel as an awesome bible or "as human a little story as paper could well carry" (115.36). Point A on the figure Dolph is about to draw, for instance, generates "O" in much the same way a prism decomposes light into its spectrum (287.7–10). The "O" can be thought of as a point, or a circle or a rainbow arc. Perhaps the triangle itself is a prism, extended as a three-dimensional object in space, even though we see only its triangular base; in that case, the circles might be two-dimensional views of three-dimensional barrels[31]—or spheres (295.4) —or domes (299.15–16) —or tops, cones, or gyres.[32] The two points of the initial "strayed line," then, can be thought of as dots, any two- or three-dimensional circular shapes, or two widening and/or retreating gyres. In the drawing given *(see Figure 3)*, we can see the two points as bicycle-wheel axles; indeed, the "two" by which the woman is known is called "our twain of doubling bicirculars" (295.30–31). If we imagine the square as a quincunx ($\vcenter{\hbox{$\cdot\,\cdot$}}$) [33] and each of the remaining three points as more wheel axles, the three-wheeled tricycle of the male, with the two-wheeled bicycle of the female, will form a five-wheeled base[34] (when transformed into a three–dimensional figure) for the "coach with the six insides,"[35] the cube formed by our **E** in all three-dimensional positions. After examining the cube in detail, we can go on to try to visualize the mirror-world and Joyce's multi-dimensioned model of the universe. The "night-lesson" is not so easy as it looks. When the tutor says, "I'll make you to see figuratleavely the whome of your eternal geomater," he means, actually, the *whole* of your "eternal" geometry.

11] *The Coach with the Sex Insides*

ALL OF *Finnegans Wake* is a "night-lesson" which can be apprehended only through the kind of medium that transcends day-logic and permits glimpses into the non-rational psychic world—that of the dream. The box that contains the universal secrets of man is as variable in size and symbolism as any of the other objects or clusters of objects in the book. At first, it is spoken of as the "cube-house" of the universe, result of the thunderously creative anal explosion of the father God (5.14–15). But it is also the father-man of the entire circling epic—Finnegan, the "solid man" (1.32), and *"Hic cubat edilis,"* the "bronto-ichthyan form outlined" (7.20–23) —as well as HCE's own pub, which, at various times, seems to roll along a railway as a boxcar, wheel down medieval roads as a wagon-stage for mystery plays,[36] sail the seas as an ark[37] or a love-bark, or cross the skies as a starry coach.[38] Usually, these various identities are deliberately confused. The closed pub in which old king Roderick O'Conor slumps down at the end of the tavern-stories chapter (II, iii) becomes a stout ship *Nansy Hans,* and then, in the very next chapter, the bride-ship carrying the new young lovers, Tristan and Isolde. As an announcement of "Ricorso" (silent pause before a new Viconian cycle) at the beginning of Book IV, the narrator says that the pub is again temporarily closed, and the passage speaks of this malthouse as if it were a cube, a

church, a railway engine (and/or a boxcar), a heavenly
coach, a ship, a wagon—and a strawberry bed.

> The vinebranch of Heremonheber . . . is leaved invert and
> fructed proper but the *cub*lic hatches endnot open yet for
> hourly rincers' mess [mass]. . . . Malthus [malthouse] is
> yet lukked in close. Withun. . . . It is not even yet the
> *engine of the load* with haled morries full of crates. . . .
> The greek Sideral Reulthway [great sidereal (Siberian;
> starry) Railway], as it havvents, will soon be starting a
> smooth [anew] with its first single hastencraft [Danish
> "hesten" == horse; hence horsepower]. Danny buzzers
> [omnibuses?] instead of the vialact coloured milk *train* on
> the fartykket [far-ticket; ship (Danish "fartyg")] plan *run*
> with its endless *gallaxi*on of rotatorattlers and the smool-
> troon our elderens rememberem as the scream of the service,
> Strubry Bess [strawberry beds; cf. 558.35–559.6]. Also the
> *waggon*wobblers are still yet everdue to precipitate [water]
> after last night's combustion [fire]. . . . Inattendance who is
> who is [two] will play that's what's that [three] to what's
> that, what [three].   (604.3–21; italics mine)

The suggestion in the early part of the passage is that
someone ("un"; Malthus) is still locked "close within" the
cube. The opening of the box, then, means an exposure of
the *person* inside. The walls are the walls of a man, and
the process of the "opening up" constitutes a major part
of the narrative of *Finnegans Wake*, as will be seen.

The frequent recurrence of the constellation image
provides strong evidence to support the idea that the cubical coach is to be identified with Ursa Major, the Bear (in
the form of the Big Dipper) and sometimes with Ursa
Minor, the Little Dipper (which is more closely associated
with the "cad"-son than with the father. This makes Ursa
Minor a "cub" instead of a cube!). The defendant at the
trial reports that he was confronted by a "revolver" and the
words, "you're shot, major" (Ursa Major). The "Way-

layer" is said to have hailed "fro' the prow [as of the ship; or The Plow: another name for the Big Dipper] of Little Britain" (Little Dipper), and is called a "crawsopper" (gracehoper-Shem). His threat was that he "would surely shoot her, the aunt,[39] by pistol, (she could be okaysure of that!) or, failing of such, bash in Patch's blank face beyond recognition" (62.31-63.5). Elsewhere, the suggested image is that of a hen banging her "bear" into proper shape: "when your pullar [pullet; polar] beer turns out Bruin [also brewin'] O'Luinn and beat his barge into a battering pram [a new name for the "coach"] with her wattling way [Milky Way; Wattling Street] for cubblin [Dublin; cub; cube]" (328.1-3).[40]

Finnegans Wake is itself a box that opens up to reveal the sins and possibilities of a man; the unopened pub hides "one within"; so the cube can be represented one more way—as a confessional where secrets are revealed. One figurative way to get at the inside of our cubical coach with the six insides is to cut the edges of the box in such a way that the square faces can be laid flat in the form of a cross. Yawn is stretched out in just such a shape at the beginning of III, iii, enabling his questioners to peer into secret recesses as if into a midden mound of the past. (*See Figure 4.*)

> The sinus the curse [sign of the cross]. That's it. Hung Chung Egglyfella now speak he tell numptywumpty topsawys belongahim pidgin. Secret things other persons place there covered not. . . . Enfilmung infirmity [eternity]. . . . And it's all us rangers you'll be facing in the box before the twelfth correctional. . . . Don Gouverneur Buckley's in the Tara Tribune, sporting the insides of a Rhutian Jhanaral. (374.33-375.24)

This is the "letter" for which one of the names is *"The Fokes Family Interior"* (106.22). So it is really the inner

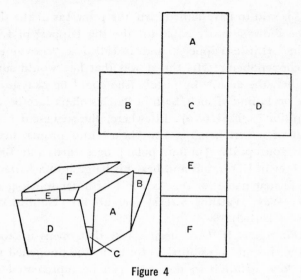

Figure 4

side of the "envelope"; there is no separation of form and
content at all. And I think Joyce makes it clear that Yawn,
sprawling in the form of a cross, is to be equated with the
cubical coach that sails as a constellation.

> Yawn! All of asprawl he was laying too amengst the pop-
> pies. . . . And it was far more similar to a satrap he lay
> there . . . all surrounded . . . like Lord *Lumen, coach*ing
> his preferred *constellations* in faith and doctrine, for old
> Matt Gregory, 'tis he had the *star*menagerie, Marcus Lyons
> and Lucas Metcalfe Tarpey and the mack that never forgave
> the ass that lurked behind him, Jonny na Hossaleen.[41]
> (476.19–28; italics mine)

And Jaun, when he recedes into the past (III, ii) , is travelling along the phosphorescent "wake" of the coach. " 'Tis
well you'll be looked after from last to first as yon beam of
light we follow receding on your photophoric pilgrimage
to your antipodes in the past, you who so often consigned

your distributory tidings of great joy into our nevertoolate-
tolove box" (472.15–19).

Laid out this way, each square face of the cube (that
is, the *inside* face) can be made to represent, geometrically,
one of the six sexual "sides" dealt with in the book. The
⊣ for Issy and ⊢ for Tristram form an **H**, a representation
of Tristram-Isolde romantic idealism *(Figure 5)*. Tristram

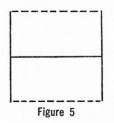

Figure 5

is (as well as a Shem-Shaun composite), the fictional hero
of Issy's imagination; he is, in reality, a projection of herself—a reversed ⊢.[42] That is probably why the Tristan-
Isolde chapter (II, iv) is dominated by the number "four,"
instead of by twos and threes. The coupling of these kissing
lovers is a two-by-two proposition, and they are watched
by the equally-limited four old lechers (each with only
half a "hat"). ⊏, in impotent union with ∧ *(Figure 6)*,

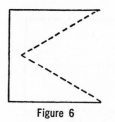

Figure 6

represents the male-female "sides" of the father, and also
the ineffectual coming together of the brothers without the
central figures to complete them.[43] There must be two
squares for the E bisecting the female triangle: one a rep-

resentation of the completed sexual act as it pertains to
HCE and ALP (*Figure 7*),[44] and the other, in an opposing

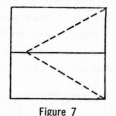

Figure 7

position, standing for the act of fornication (with the
"two" in the park) (*Figure 8*).[45] Up against the *back* of

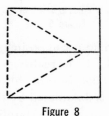

Figure 8

this latter **E** (around a corner of the cube?) is the **E** without the triangle (*Figure 9*), the one symbolizing the act
of sodomy of the three soldiers.[46]. This leaves one square

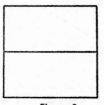

Figure 9

for the mirror-love narcissism of Issy,[47] a triangle bisected
by her symbol, (*Figure 10*). Narcissism, impotence, romantic love, fornication, homosexuality, and fruitful com-

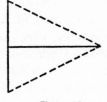

Figure 10

pletion: collectively, these symbols represent every activity
of man in history—wars, art, city-building, religion, loves—
his whole self-development through error and success. Joyce
may have scoffed at Freud and Jung, but Freud's influence
is unmistakable in this use of sexual metaphor.

Yawn as a cross, however, can hardly be contemplated
only as a two-dimensional figure. He lies as a "crossroads
puzzler," his "length by breadth nonplussing his thickness,"[48] and his "bellyvoid of nebulose with his neverstop
navel." The "nebulousness" of his thickness is partly explained by his extension into the starry atmosphere. His
hair is "cometshair"; he has "asteroid knuckles, ribs and
members"; and his veins are like shooting stars. Moreover,
the "four claymen," like an angelic choir, as well as like
an inquiring group of judges, climb from "all their cardinal parts" to "hold their sworn starchamber quiry on
him" (475.3–19). The paths the four travel are through
time, and the scene about to be enacted is a "drama para-
polylogic" (474.5), indicating that the real figure to be
contemplated may be polyhedral, with dimensions beyond
the logic of this world. If Yawn, as an opened box, is a
cross *with thickness,* how can he be folded up into a cube?
And yet the four are "cooched [allusion to the coach] down
a mamalujo by his cubical crib" (476.31–32), in the formation of a tetrahedron,[49] rather than as points of a two-
dimensional square.

The answer is hidden in the trial chapter, in a passage which reveals Joyce's fascination with the mysterious intimations surrounding theories of the fourth dimension and non-Euclidean geometry, which accompanied the introduction of the theory of relativity.[50] The material explaining such concepts is certainly difficult for a non-mathematical mind (like mine) to comprehend fully, and yet an attempt at understanding will open up new areas for further appreciation of the occult qualities pertaining to the sexual theme, which Joyce apparently felt he could introduce into a novel through the medium of the dream.

> Wherefore let it hardly . . . be said . . . that the prisoner of that sacred edifice . . . was at his best a onestone parable, a rude breathing on the void of to be [the future], a venter hearing his own bauchspeech [fart; smoke language (spirit talk)] in backwords [words of the past; reversed-in-time words; backwards], or . . . but tristurned [Tristan-ed; three-times-turned] initials, the cluekey to a worldroom beyond the roomwhorld [the fourth dimension], for scarce one . . . cared seriously or for long to doubt . . . (the gravitational pull perceived by certain fixed residents and the capture of uncertain comets chancedrifting through our system suggesting an authenticitatem of his aliquitudinis) the canonicity of his existence as a tesseract.[51] (100.24–35)

A tesseract is a four-dimensional hypercube which cannot be graphically represented in three-dimensional space unless it is depicted in three-dimensional terms, e.g., as "unfolded" in the same way a three-dimensional cube is opened out into a cross. (*See Figure 11.*) [52] It consists of eight cubes, which are generated by the movement of all points of a three-dimensional cube in four-space—just the way a three-dimensional cube is generated by the movement of a two-dimensional square in three-space in a direction perpendicular to its two dimensions. (*See Figure 12.*) The difficulty is that we have no other visually perceptible dimensions than the three of length, breath, and thickness. So

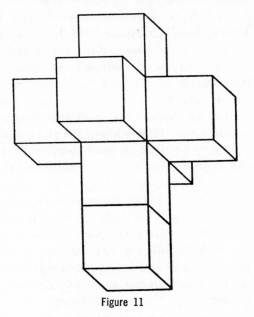

Figure 11

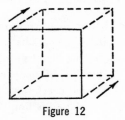

Figure 12

we are unable to imagine the direction that any cube could take at right angles to itself—in a direction perpendicular to its three dimensions. We can look at the eight cubes laid out in our three-dimensional world, but to *see* Finnegan's "wake"—the path that the box makes as it becomes a tesseract—is an impossibility, unless we can imagine a mysterious mirror-world, where a solid object might be able to rotate about a *plane* rather than about a line, and where lines of movement would pass right out of our three-dimensional space into inscrutable realms. ALP writes that "we were treated not very grand when the police and everybody is all bowing to us when we go out in all directions on Wanterlond Road with my cubarola glide" (618.20–22). The box we see (and it must be remembered that the cube is the man) may be just the tail of the original comet (HCE without the glory of a mythical giant), or it may be the only manifestation of a tesseract that can be apprehended in a three-dimensional world, a "cross"-section of a four-dimensional body, a mere projection of the real shape. If our entire universe is made analogous to the two-dimensional plane, like the surface of a lake which divides a real world and a mirror world, whatever is seen in the dividing space-plane may be only a hint of what projects above and below (although the two terms "above" and "below" do not accurately describe unknowable directions of the fourth dimension).

The mirror-lake analogy is used over and over in *Finnegans Wake*. In Madame Toshowus's museum,

> many have paused before that exposure of him by old Tom Quad, a flashback in which he sits sated, gowndabout, in clericalease habit, watching bland sol slithe dodgsomely into the nethermore, a globule of maugdleness about to corrugitate his mild dewed cheek and the tata of a tiny victorienne, Alys, pressed by his limper looser.   (57.23–29)

When one reflects that a three-dimensional being can see right into the center of a two-dimensional object—say, a square—one can understand Joyce's interest in a four-dimensional world where a being might penetrate with ease the dark inside-world of the three-dimensional human, might be able to see all six sides (twelve, if we count interior as well as exterior) of the cube at once.[53]

The old men appear to represent the fourth dimension much of the time. They are alluded to as "old thalasso-crats of invinsible empores [invisible empires], maskers of the waterworld, facing one way to another way and this way on that way, from severalled their fourdimmansions. Where the lighning leaps from the numbulous; where coold by cawld breide lieth langwid; the bounds wherein-bourne our solied [solar] bodies all attomed attaim arrest: appoint, that's all" (367.25–30). As they hover around the bride-ship (II, iv), they are outside of the box ("peering in . . . through the steamy windows, into the honeymoon cabins": 395.7–9), and yet they are set about in perpendicu-lar directions from the cube's three dimensions, watching the "cubin" as if it were a point in the center of a quin-cunx. ("And it was a fiveful moment for the poor old time-tetters, ticktacking, in tenk the count": 396.26–28.) They reminisce about the "otherworld" (385.4) and complain that "The new world presses" (387.36). So it does. The shift from the old king on the inside of the pub (II, iii) to the four watchers on the outside of the cabin is a shift in perspective. The king is down, but the keying (kissing) begins all over again, and the image supporting the change is a telescoping of the three-dimensional world to a point, so that it may travel along the line (s) of the fourth di-mension.

Joyce felt, I am sure, that dreams give us a hint of the occult; a man, because he considers only his waking life "real," comprises a dualism—one "being" living in the ordinary time-and-space world and the other belonging to some other world. Such a dualism is represented by Berkeley and St. Patrick in the debate over the "illusionary" and the "real" world. Berkeley, defending the night world, says that "fallen man" sees "but one photoreflection of the several [seven: 'heptachromatic sevenhued septicoloured'] iridals gradationes of solar light, that one which that part of it . . . had shown itself . . . unable to absorbere, whereas for numpa one puraduxed seer in seventh degree of wisdom of Entis-Onton he savvy inside true inwardness of reality, the Ding hvad [thing what] in idself id est [Freudian terms], all objects . . . allside showed themselves in trues coloribus resplendent with sextuple [six sexual sides] gloria of light actually retained . . . inside them" (611.16–24). "Rumnant Patholic" (St. Patrick) is limited to a stereoptican ("stareotypopticus") day view, the kind that makes even a dualism seem like a unity. He sees only the Irish world, and it is green. King Leary's head is green, and his six-colored clothes are all the color of boiled spinach ("his essixcoloured holmgrewnworsteds costume the his fellow saffron pettikilt look same hue of boiled spinasses": 611.35–36) ; his "readyrainroof" is green, his eyes the color of thyme and parsley, and he has an olive-green ring on his finger (612.9–10) . At the end of the argument, there is no victory of one contender over the other. The scene ends in sodomy. "Bilkilly-Belkelly-Balkally" (the "three") "shuck his thumping fore [front; four-dimensional] features apt the hoyhop of His Ards" (612.34–35) .

On occasion, the ego subconsciously senses that the realm of these "multimathematical immaterialities" constitutes "reunited selfdom . . . in the higherdimissional selfless Allself" (394.31–395.2) , but the irony is that "reality" cannot be defined by one kind of "world" apart from the other. The impotence implied in the symbols for the twins, ⊏ and ∧, automatically cancels out any unqualified assertions that the "union" of Shem and Shaun is a true synthesis of opposites. The crossing of their paths, or the meeting symbolized by their homosexuality, is a union which is to be accepted just for what it is: a temporary confrontation of forces which still continue to move in contradictory orbits. The difference between fruitful and unfruitful sexual union is not a moral distinction nor even a distinction of expedience. Man-woman sex of the prop-

agating kind simply produces seeds of continuance as op-
posed to crossings of conflict. Although war is impotent
as a forward-moving impetus, it is inevitable. In very general categories, the war between Shem (Berkeley) and
Shaun (St. Patrick) is between art and religion. The permanently constructive union of these two factors, according to the symbols of impotence, seems an impossibility.
On the other hand, Joyce's use of these opposites to depict
the dichotomy in a single Shem-Shaun individual demonstrates his understanding of a perpetual, insoluble paradox
existing in every human being.[54]

The dark aesthetic world often appears to take two
directions, one into the past and the other into the future,
so that the soul of man becomes a "battlefield of the past
and the future."[55] In *Finnegans Wake*, the rear sexual encounter signifies the past, but, since it is a forward experience for one of the partners, there is the indication that
the past will be repeated in the future, just as the forward
encounter with the "girls"—part of the memory-burden of
guilt—will also become a future sin. The woman digging
up the "letter" is both exposing and rescuing, with an
impetus steadily forward in time. And conflict runs through
all the cycles because of man's implicit dualism. The three-
dimensional cube which represents the "now" of the day
world is the only manifestation of the tesseract—the total
man—in the three-dimensional universe. Whatever shadowy
reflections of other dimensions are apprehended can be
glimpsed only in dreams or in art. In *Finnegans Wake*, different levels of the dream manifest greater dimensions of
reality, just as the dark world of the genitals reveals the
secrets of the psyche.

Joyce's universe goes through cycles of expansion and
contraction which correspond, on a sexual level, with erection and detumescence, and on a literary level with the
undulatory shifts from word to world and back again.

Synecdoche provides a stylistic analogue for the molecular activity which takes place when matter changes state, and for shifting perceptions caused by the phenomenon of relativity. It also allows Joyce to move, at will, from the sublime to the ridiculous, from broad universal applications to homely little anecdotes, from lofty symbolic overtones to dirty jokes. The art is the unfailing humor of bathos. Thus, a fart can be made the "Ghazi Power" (521.22) which becomes the "explosion" of civilization. From a point (the sexual "one," and thus a "zero" dimension), the world gets larger and larger, its molecules not only separating in three-dimensional directions but also moving along the dimension of time, until, as with Yeats' gyres, "things fall apart; the center cannot hold" ("The Second Coming"). Then it is time for the "implosion," the "exprogressive process":

> Our wholemole millwheeling vicociclometer, a tetradomational gazebocroticon[56] (the Mamma Lujah" known to every schoolboy scandaller . . .), autokinatonetically preprovided with a clappercoupling smeltingworks exprogressive process [note the synaesthesia which helps the synthesis], (for the farmer, his son and their homely codes, known as eggburst, eggblend, eggburial and hatch-as-hatchcan) receives through a portal vein [door; portage; postal] the dialytically [dual, dialectic, analytic (anal)] separated elements of precedent decomposition for the verypetpurpose of subsequent recombination so that the *h*eroticisms [heroics; eroticisms], *c*atastrophes and *e*ccentricities transmitted by the *a*ncient *l*egacy of the *p*ast [ALP gathering and transmitting through the recombined letter], type by tope, letter from litter, word at ward, with sendence of sundance[57] . . . all, anastomosically[58] assimilated and preteridentified paraidiotically,[59] in fact, the sameold gamebold adomic [atomic; Adam-ic] structure of our Finnius the old One [back to the anal point], as highly charged with electrons as hophazards can effective it, may be there for you, Cocka-

looralooraloomenos, when cup, platter and pot come piping hot, as sure as herself pits hen to paper[60] and there's scribings scrawled on eggs [X].   (614.27–615.10; italics mine)

Because the universe changes in size according to the size of the observer, the speed of his perception, and the observation point, its dimensional identity changes too. The fourth dimension is non-spatial for us as three-dimensional creatures. We have come to accept time as the fourth dimension though we do not perceive a visual, tactile track left by movement in time. But Joyce can make us imagine that "wake" if he is at liberty to reduce the entire three-dimensional universe to a point, for "any space solid, up to the *infinite sphere* of old physics, is a *point* or a *moment* when taken in time."[61] And, if the space-time continuum is curved, as Joyce and his contemporaries were assured that it was, we can certainly imagine our "coach" travelling on the three-dimensional surface of some immense four-dimensional sphere (circling the square; squaring the circle). Moreover, if *that* image is reduced to a point, we can easily grant the existence of a fifth dimension. The expansion and the reduction possibilities are infinite.

So Kevin, as a point, sits alone as a self-satisfied god of the zero-dimensional "Pointland"[62] in the center of the Irish universe (605–606); the Earwicker family interact as two-dimensional symbols and sometimes sense the ghostly existence of other worlds; the cubical coach wheels around the globe and shoots like a comet through the air; and the four-dimensional "mamalujo" opens up a hypercube so that our three-dimensional eyes might be able to see that the boundaries of our universe are merely the limitations of our day-world perceptions. Shem ponders the teasing concept of infinity in the long parenthesis inserted into the "lessons" chapter:

and, an you could peep inside the cerebralised saucepan [dipper] of this eer illwinded goodfornobody, you would see in his house of thoughtsam (was you, that is, decontaminated enough to look discarnate) what a jetsam litterage of convolvuli of times lost or strayed, of lands derelict and of tongues laggin too, longa yamsayore, not only that but, search lighting, beached, bashed and beaushelled *à la Mer* pharahead into faturity, your own convolvulis pickninnig capman would real [reel] to jazztfancy the novo takin place of what stale words whilom were woven with and fitted fairly featly for, so; and equally so . . . it is that, whenas the swiftshut scareyss of our pupilteachertaut duplex will hark back to lark to you symibellically that, though a day be as dense as a decade, no mouth has the might to set a mearbound to the march of a landsmaul, in half a sylb, helf a solb, holf a salb onward the beast of boredom, common sense, lurking gyrographically down inside his loose Eating S. S. collar is gogoing of whisth to you sternly how—Plutonic loveliaks twinnt Platonic yearlings—you must, how, in undivided reawlity draw the line somewhawre (292.12–32)

In *Finnegans Wake*, Joyce's static art, which he held to firmly, even though he outgrew the puerile limitations of Stephen Dedalus, is shown to be static only in terms of our naturally restricted understanding. Geometry of the kind not logically grasped by the daytime mind is essential to Joyce's intention, I think, to comment not only about art—as Stephen Dedalus did—but about all of life and man's position in it. I find it hard to believe that Joyce played mathematical games in this book merely to amuse himself and to confound his readers. His toying with mystical numbers, letters, and shapes enables him to show that what seems reasonably firm and static is, in fact, relatively unstable: alive, moving, changing, reshaping, continuing. What do the propositions that there is no such thing as a straight line or a central fixed point "say" to people? What implications are there in the suggestion that a circle or a semi-circular rainbow is divided into seven equal parts? Or that the boundaries of our vision reveal to us only a partial and erroneous view of a cross? It seems to me that the very method of *Finnegans Wake* damns all dogma, scientific or religious, putting us out to float in the limitless expanse of uncertainty and change. On the other hand, the serio-comic social homeliness represented by the ever-dying, ever-rising phallus provides an easily recognizable constant for us to "cling to . . . as with drowning hands" (119.3) amid the ever-flowing protean language of our prank-playing captain. If *Finnegans Wake* is a big dirty joke, it is the cosmic joke of the universe, a universe accepted by Joyce and acceptable to those readers who see affirmation in an unreliability artfully ordered by a whimsical craftsman. Since it would appear unwise to pin Joyce down any more strictly than this, I am content, with Shem, to arbitrarily "draw the line somewhawre."

Punkt.

NOTES/INDEX

NOTES

Introduction

[1] (New York: The Viking Press, 1968), pp. 11; 41–42.

[2] *A Wake Newslitter*, New Series, Vol. II, No. 2 (April, 1965), 3–8; continued in No. 3 (June, 1965), 21–25; No. 4 (August, 1965), 24–27; No. 6 (December, 1965), 17–22; concluded in Vol. III, No. 1 (February, 1966), 6–14.

[3] (New York: Vintage Books, 1961), p. 697.

[4] Citations from *Finnegans Wake* are taken from The Viking Press edition (New York, 1967).

1 THREE TIMES IS A CHARM

1] *The Prankquean*

[5] "Cry not yet! There's many a smile to Nondum. . . . for every busy eerie whig's a bit of a torytale to tell. One's upon a thyme and two's behind their lettice leap and three's among the strubbely beds. . . . Of a noarch and a chopwife; of a pomme full grave and a fammy of levity; or of golden youths that wanted gelding; or of what the mischievmiss made a man do" (20.19–31).

[6] *A Second Census of Finnegans Wake* (Northwestern University Press, 1963), pp. 192–93.

[7] See 89.3–4, alluding to the "dreamyums" (dromios; twins) "both as like as a duel of lentils? Peacisely." This passage occurs in a context which includes "showeradown" (88.32), "Portterand" (88.33), Eve, fire, water, and door: "A stoker temptated by evesdripping aginst the driver" (89.1).

[8] "Finegale" identifies Jarl van Hoother with Finn MacCool, whose name in one Irish form—"fiongal"—means fratricide or murder (Glasheen, *Second Census*, p. 81).

⁹ For a short summary of the legend, see Glasheen, *Second Census,* p. 64.

¹⁰ For a more exhaustive analysis of the connotative qualities of the language in this story, see Bernard Benstock, *Joyce-Again's Wake* (Seattle, 1965), pp. 267–96. Mr. Benstock also attaches major significance to the urinary process in the tale, and says that it "is certainly second in importance to the sexual, although Joyce allows no real distinction between the two." His comments give importance, as well, to the reviving qualities of the female "flow." However, we do not agree in his stressing, through the masturbation images, the "impotence" of the Jarl, nor can I be satisfied with his insistence that neither this story nor the account of the sins in the park indicates "any act of sexual aggression."

¹¹ Other associations with the Flood: "floody, flatuous world"; rainbow ("arkway of Trihump"); the references to porter and drinking (Noah supposedly was the first vintner); forty years' "walk," raining (cf. forty days' and forty nights' rain in the Bible story).

¹² Glasheen: " 'Whiskey' comes from Ir. *uisge,* or 'water;' Irish whiskey is usquebaugh, or *uisgebeathe,* 'water of life.' Water and strong-waters are never really distinct in *FW*" ("The Opening Paragraphs," *A Wake Newslitter,* New Series, Vol. II, No. 3 (June, 1965), 21).

¹³ Although Shem is said to be "in a state of hopelessly helpless intoxication" (171.7) and is referred to as "sousy" (173.1), "soggert" (174.25), "badly the worse for boosegas" (176.31), etc., his indulgences include "no likedbylike firewater" (171.13); "He would not put fire to his cerebrum; he would not throw himself in Liffey" (172.18–19). He was, as a matter of fact, "Fireless" (172.25).

¹⁴ Armor has at least a double reference: to the male member in erection and to Sir Armory Tristram, invader-founder associated with the St. Lawrence family of Howth (Glasheen, *Second Census,* p. 260). Shaun's use of the word, moreover, leads one to suspect a third meaning which substantiates the idea that, throughout *Finnegans Wake,* Shaun's sexualism is non-productive: "armor" is an eighteenth-century euphemism for condom and was so regarded by Stephen in the Circe episode of *Ulysses,* when he misquoted Swift's epigram.

¹⁵ Clive Hart has called attention to the sexual connotations in the passage pertaining to ALP on 201.19–20: "to feale the

gay aire of my salt troublin bay and the race of the saywint up me ambushure" ("my hole" in an early draft) . A reason for the male having to "git the wind up." *Structure and Motif in Finnegans Wake* (Evanston: Northwestern University Press, 1962) , p. 204.

16 I have italicized "kertssey," because ALP as the tailor's daughter is one connection between the Prankquean and the Norwegian Captain stories. See part 1, chapter 3.

17 Besides "magistrate," this word connotes "maggies T rape" (see part 2, discussion of the "T"), and "majesty rape"—mutual between king and queen.

18 *FW* 372.3–5 has been cited by several scholars as proof that Issy is the Prankquean, but that passage refers to the tailor's daughter, who is not the same as HCE's daughter, although she stands in the same relation as the young temptress, Issy.

2] *The Game of Colours*

19 Joyce's letter to Harriet Weaver, November 22, 1930. *Letters of James Joyce,* ed. Stuart Gilbert (London, 1957) , p. 295.

20 Parallels to the biographical details of Stephen Dedalus (and, in a measure, of Joyce himself) can be recognized in each of Glugg's actions in the game. A rather thorough explication of the action is here given, since the chapter provides an excellent example of Joyce's use of linguistic puzzles.

21 I feel certain that the "troopers" in "holytroopers" refer to the "privates" of the son. Cf. Shaun in his "sunflower state" with a "shapeless hat" and "haliodraping het" on page 509—"hat" referring here to the tip of the phallus or perhaps to a condom.

22 The "real presence" imagery in this passage heightens the travesty of Glugg's trying to impersonate the Father.

23 That some kind of trick is intended is suggested by an allusion to Chaucer's *Miller's Tale.* These are the same words Absolon used to Nicholas (whom he believed to be Alison) in the dark, just before he branded Nicholas's "erse."

24 This progression recalls the relationship of the dummy to the young Prankquean and perhaps confirms the contention that the dummy (or dolly) is a model of the damsel to be. Cf. the "storiella" chapter (II, ii) , where "gramma" refers to her presexual days as the time when she was "grappa's" intellectual pick-me-up pigmy—"his analectual pygmyhop" (268.28–29; an anal

connotation is included). And Issy's note adds: "A washable lovable floatable doll" (268, n. 7).

25 Alludes to Lyons' English teahouses, and to *The Lady of Lyons*, a Bulwer-Lytton play. Cf. James S. Atherton, *The Books at the Wake* (New York: The Viking Press, 1960), p. 109.

26 A paragraph from Edgar Quinet (*Introduction à la philosophie de l'histoire de l'humanité*, in *Oeuvres Complètes*, Vol. II [Paris, 1857], 367–68), French historian, which Joyce uses as motif throughout *Finnegans Wake*. The parody most nearly like the original is on FW 281.

27 The paragraph announcing the appearance of the moon carries numerous allusions to Jewish festivals, all of which are dated according to the New Moon. Seder (Joyce's spelling: Ceder; Neomenie = New Moon) is the prescribed evening ceremony of Pesach, the Spring Passover festival celebrating the passing of the angel of death over the houses of the Jews whose doors were marked with the blood of a lamb sacrifice. Clues to Joyce's use of the allusion here can be found in the traditional ritual, which is divided in three parts: first, the questioning of the father by the youngest son regarding the meaning of the celebration and the customs accompanying it; next the blessing and eating of prescribed foods, terminating with the eating of *afikomon*, "the half-matsoh" that the father has hidden so that the children may not find it and steal it away from him; lastly, prayers and songs, and the pouring of a cup of wine for Elijah, the looked-for forerunner of the messiah, during which time the door is opened for the prophet to come in and eat and drink. Although the children fall asleep, the elder members of the family continue to sit about and sing.

The autumn festival of Sukkos, also alluded to by the reference to the *lulov* branches (palm branches), includes the Feast of Tabernacles, when meals are taken outside in booths (*sukkos*) open to the sky. During Sukkos, a libation of water is added to the libation of wine which is poured on the altar daily. The priest holds the ewer of water over the altar, and the people call out to him to hold it higher so they can see he is not pouring it on the ground. (The feminine "water," mixed with wine, is the "coverfew" or covering of fire, in Joyce's allusion.) The *lulov* is a phallic symbol of fertility; the Sukkos celebration was originally a nature festival, connected with the celebration of the gathering of the crops.

Joyce alludes to the Sedar feast (which includes the children's questioning of the father, their attempts to steal his authority, and the open door), and also to the Feast of Tabernacles, the celebration of fertility, when the children's play is over ("Shopshup. . . . 'tis time for bairns ta hame": 244.6–9) and the parents, especially the father, are in full power.

Another ceremony is interesting to the analogy: at the end of Sukkos, the children traditionally dismember the *lolovim* and eat the citron which accompanies the palm-branch bundles. All this information was gathered from Hayyim Schauss, *The Jewish Festivals,* tr. by Samuel Jaffe (Cincinnati, 1938), p. 75ff, 182ff, 274ff.

[28] For what they are worth, here are a few translations:

Rose = (Germ.) rose; (Med. Germ.) erysipelas
Band = (Germ.) ribbon; bond
Bande = (Germ.) band, company, gang
Swarthants = swarthy hands? black ants?
Sheidan = (Germ. scheiden) divorce; (Germ. Scheide) vagina

The first color referred to is apparently rose or red; the second is black (like a chimney sweep); the third I haven't been able to figure out.

[29] Their confusion is compounded for the reader a dozen times by the various possible interpretations of these hybrid words. Besides "orthodox," "artthoudux" can include "Art thou a leader?" (Latin "dux" = "leader"), some suggestion of the same meaning in a connotation of "authority," a reference to Arthur, the legendary upright king (cf. "orthotropic," meaning "tending to grow vertically"). But straight-line vertical progression can also suggest homosexuality or narcissism. "Heterotropic," on the other hand, connotes variety—the heterosexuality of the normal meeting of sexual opposites— and is in such close proximity to the heliotrope riddle that it immediately suggests the male-female union that Izod desires. Yet it also carries overtones of perversion, since "heterotopia" means the "misplacement of an organ or part of the body" (Dictionary).

[30] See 302.31–303.2 and Issy's Note 1 (p. 303): "And ook, ook, ook, fanky! All the charictures in the drame! This is how San holypolypools [Kev]. And this, pardonsky! is the way Romeopullupalleaps [Dolph].[1]" "[1]He, angel that I thought him, and he not aebel to speel eelyotripes., Mr Tellibly Divilcult!"

[31] Sure enough, on the bottom of the same page, the language

reverts to such baby-talk distortion: "As a gololy bit to joss? Leally and tululy."

[32] The flower-girls open and turn to him "in heliolatry, so they may catchcup in their calyzettes, alls they go troping, those parryshoots from his muscalone pistil, for he can eyespy through them, to their selfcolours" (237.1–4). The twenty-eight girls, seeing Shaun kick himself into action in the Jaun chapter (III, ii), call him their "concelebrated meednight sunflower, piopadey boy, their solase in dorckaness" (470.6–7).

[33] For confirmation of these contentions, cf. the homosexual overtones in 281.14–15, and the words of woe—transformed to Maori "Au! Au!"—in proximity to "hyacinths" on 335.4. "Ai, Ai" appears in another form on 456.7.

[34] Kate, regarding this encounter, mutters, "Blusterboss, blowharding about all he didn't do. Hell o' your troop!" (273.23–25).

3] *The Captain, and the Russian General*

[35] ALP power, "lackslipping along as if their liffing deepunded on it" (310.5–6).

[36] See Glasheen, *Second Census,* p. 138, for the story attributed to John Joyce.

[37] It is amusing to speculate upon the extent to which Joyce was influenced by Proust's depiction of a homosexual tailor, Jupien (*Cities of the Plain*). The first encounter between Jupien and M. de Charlus includes conversation concerning a possible prior acquaintance in Zurich, as well as an invitation to activities behind a closed door. " 'Come inside, you shall have everything you require,' said the tailor. . . . The door of the shop closed behind them." (Scott Moncrieff trans.)

[38] Cf. *Ulysses,* p. 737:
"He rests. He has travelled.
With?
Sinbad the Sailor and Tinbad the Tailor . . ."

[39] The ship's husband (*hus* = house [Norwegian]) is apparently the protector or steward wife. He is referred to as "his lady her master" (311), "her wife's lairdship" (312), "good mothers gossip" (316), "shop's housebound" (317), "his wife's hopesend" (320), and "ship's gospfather" (325). The lady, then, is like a ship to be anchored, or "hooked," in nautical slang. (A "hook" is also a trap, a hinge of a door, or a bend in a river.)

[40] "Sooterkins" are imps, and so refer to possible offspring; but "sowterkins" probably means, as well, "kin of the suitor." Cf. Issy's note on 301.31: "And she [the "feacemaker's" "fancyflame" (301.4–5)] had to seek a pond's apeace to salve her suiterkins. Sued!"

[41] The "beddest his friend's" appellation, "Ahorror" (and A'Hara, Horace, acarra, ahorace, aaherra) is derived from Irish "a chara" which means "Dear" or "Friend," as in the salutation of a letter. The tailor's name is Kersse. "Ahorror" also suggests "whore," in both English and Norwegian (*hore*).

[42] Although the language of the ritual is dense, I am certain that the four-part ditty, repeated with variations throughout the book, signifies the homosexual event: "He spit in his faist (beggin) : he tape the raw baste (paddin) : he planked his pledge (as dib is a dab) : and he tog his fringe sleeve (buthock lad, fur whale) " (311.31–33) .

[43] It is evident here that the shutting of the door heralds fall and death as well as new birth and procreation.

[44] "I will speak but three ones, sayd he . . . poles a port and zones asunder, tie up in hates and repeat at luxure" (328.7–9); "The soul of everyelsesbody rolled into its oleoleself" (329.18–19) .

[45] "—Nansense, you snorsted? he was haltid considerable agenst all religions overtrow so hworefore the thokkurs pokker the bigbug miklamanded storstore exploder would he be whulesalesolde daadooped by Priest Gudfodren of the sacredhaunt suit in Diaeblen-Balkley at Domnkirk Saint Petricksburg?" (326.21–25). The Scandinavian elements in this passage are multiple. See, for actual spelling of Danish and Norwegian words, D. B. Christiani, *Scandinavian Elements of Finnegans Wake* (Evanston: Northwestern University Press, 1965) , and also Björn Tysdahl and Clive Hart, "Norwegian Captions," *A Wake Newslitter*, New Series, Vol. II, No. 2 (April, 1965) , pp. 14–15. Some loose translations are:

> haltid: always
> overtrow: superstition
> hworefore the thokkurs pokker: why the devil
> miklamanded: great man
> storstore: big, large
> daadooped: baptized
> Gudfodren: God the father
> Domnkirk: cathedral

46 The language suggests trickery by both raven and dove aspects of the female "two." This time, however, the lady was helped by the tailor's deviousness. The captain's guilt in the affair hangs on his neck like the Ancient Mariner's albatross. See 137.22–23: "by stealth of a kersse her aulburntress abaft his nape she hung."

47 *Second Census*, p. 39.

48 Cf. Biblical account of Ham's witnessing the nakedness of Noah, Gen. 9:22.

49 The name "Pukkelson" provides a link with the captain-and-tailor story, and indicates that the "son of a hump" refers to the penis as well as to the son of a humpbacked father.

50 An early draft says, "I thought he was going to high mass, Russian General" (David Hayman, ed. *A First-Draft Version of Finnegans Wake* [University of Texas Press, 1963], p. 183). Indeed, ritualistic language pervades this section, and the whole passage can be read as if it were Stephen Dedalus admitting how impossible it was, at first, for him to "kill" in himself his "father," the Roman Catholic church.

51 The language recalls Joyce's meeting with the older Yeats, to whom he is reported to have said that they had met too late for Joyce to do Yeats any good. "I met with whom it was too late. My fate! O Hate! Fairwail!" (345.13–14). See also 37.13–14 for the too early–too late connection with the meeting of the cad and HCE.

52 The plural pronoun "we" includes the other son, who, after all, is merely the Shaun side of Shem. The religious allusions serve always to involve Shaun in the father-overthrow, for he is the pious aspect of the son which is concerned with taking over the godly power of the father, just as the Shem aspect is preoccupied with surmounting the father sexually.

53 This spelling of "shot him" connects the act with the shutting of the door. The moment of sexual union is intended to be the beginning of new life for the one who "shoots" the father and replaces him. But, for the father-figure, the shut door sounds the old ruler's knell: "till Bockleyshuts the rahjahn gerachknell and regnumrockery roundup" (388.33–34).

54 The similarity of "shutter reshottus" to "sartor resartus" links the action to the "suit" story of the captain and tailor; both include symbolic homosexual events. "Sieger besieged" reminds one of the Prankquean story and, along with "shutter reshottus,"

points up the paradoxical nature of all these illustrations: The offender is the defender (cf. the ambiguous use of the word "fender" throughout *Finnegans Wake*); the shooter is shot; the knocker at the door can also be the opener or the shutter or the one behind the shut door, depending upon which way he is regarded at any given time: "who struck Buckley . . . every school-filly . . . knows . . . it was Buckleyself (we need no blooding paper to tell it neither) who struck and the Russian generals, da! da!, instead of Buckley who was caddishly struck by him when be herselves" (101.15–22).

55 The theme of outsider-invader of Ireland is here incorporated; but, again, the "counterination of shorpshoopers" refers not only to England, the "nation of shopkeepers," the invading, Buckley-type sharpshooters, but also to the England threatened with invasion by the French "fiercemarchands"—Napoleon vs. Wellington.

56 In one possible reading, this refers to the window of the outhouse. He is reading as he sits on the stool. See Christiani (*Scandinavian Elements,* p. 80) for further suggestions regarding this scene. The sliding door may also refer to the panel which separates the bar from the snug in an Irish pub, or to a part of the confession box. The passage may be read in several ways.

4] *The Door*

57 It may be, too, that Issy's mirror is a looking-glass door which must be crossed before the daughter can enter the world of the mother—or resolve her many personalities into one productive unit.

58 See 508.33: Artists at clever "spilling" (their micturition and also their provocation of the spilling of the male "tea" [See part 2]); also artists of the harp and piano (Danish "Klaver-spil" = piano playing).

2 THE LETTER

5] *T*

1 An "upandown ladder" (125.14).

2 See, below, discussion of the "T" in connection with the *Book of Kells.*

3 Clive Hart, in *Structure and Motif,* claims that the P. S. is

"a flow of urine" (p. 206) ; however, after the discussion on "tea" which follows, I think it will be found that there is little disagreement between us.

⁴ It should be evident, then, that the T as "letter" can be both the postscript and, in a larger sense, the "body" of the letter, too, because the phallus, in *Finnegans Wake,* stands for "man." It should also be clear that the letter T somehow includes the whole family—not just the males. So Issy is a ⊣; Tristan is a ⊢; even ALP will fit on its frame, as will be seen later.

⁵ *Books,* p. 63. When Shaun is asked who gave him a postmaster's permit, he says, "I have it from whowho but Hagios Colleenkiller's prophecies" (409.27–28).

⁶ See 453.19: "May my tunc fester if ever I see such a miry lot of maggalenes!" Also, what took place at the fall of the "overlisting eshtree" is said to be "tunc committed" (504.11) .

⁷ Joyce makes a large **C** in N**C**R, since it serves for two C's on the Tunc page of the *Book of Kells*: TUNCCRu are the letters on the top line.

⁸ *Books,* p. 197. Various of the titles listed on pp. 104–7 of *Finnegans Wake* are applicable to the suppositions which follow here.

⁹ Joyce's passage on form and content (FW 109) is applicable to his book and to literature as a whole, as well as to the justification for his use of such tabooed forms as the human genitals through which to present a revolutionary kind of communication.

¹⁰ According to Christiani (*Scandinavian Elements*) , "Fjorgn" includes both Odin and Jord (Earth) , and is both masculine and feminine. Here, it is also a Gaelic and Norse mixture for Finn MacCool. "Camhelsson" combines "Gammel" (old) and son. "Kvindes" = "women's" (and of course "queen's" is also included in "Kvinnes") ; "Soldru's men" are the three privates.

6] *Tree*

¹¹ Cf. *"Treestam"* (104.10) ; "treestem" (424.28) ; "Treestone" (113.19).

¹² See 235.28: "T" stands for penis and "I sold U" for vagina in the passage, "T will be waiting for uns as I sold U [woman is always associated with betrayal] at the first antries [entry; but also a completing of the word "Tristan"—tries-T-an]."

¹³ Cf. the letter as a "jungle of woods" (112.4) .

[14] "Listeneth! 'Tis a tree story. How olave, that firile, was aplantad in her liveside. How tannoboom held tonobloom" (564.21–23).

[15] "What secondtonone myther rector and maximost bridgesmaker was the first to rise taller through his beanstale than the bluegum buaboababbaun or the giganteous Wellingtonia Sequoia" (126.10–12).

[16] "I askt you, dear lady, to judge on my tree by our fruits. I gave you of the tree. . . . My freeandies, my celeberrimates: my happy bossoms, my allfalling fruits of my boom" (535.31–34).

[17] "That bloasted tree. Forget not the felled!" (340.8).

[18] May 24, 1924, *Letters*, p. 214.

[19] Of course, sexual connotations pervade all of these "religious" references. "I'm leaving my darling proxy behind for your consolering, lost Dave the Dancekerl. . . . He's the mightiest penumbrella I ever flourished on behond the shadow of a post" (462.16–22).

[20] Cf. the church, the "bride of Christ": "This is me aunt Julia Bride, your honour, dying to have you languish to scandal in her bosky old delltangle" (465.1–3). "Take her out of poor tuppeny luck before she goes off in pure treple licquidance. I'd give three shillings a pullet to the canon for the conjugation to shadow you kissing her from me leberally all over as if she was a crucifix" (465.22–26).

[21] "Zin"; "Zinzin." (I do not try to refute what anyone else has said about this recurrent insertion in the text; I merely call attention to one of its important meanings here.)

[22] The diction introducing the tree makes certain that the connection with Yggdrasil and Norse mythology is established. Four harts, which constantly bit the buds of Yggdrasil's branches, represented the four winds. "Woful Dane Bottom" relates the tree to Woden (for which "Ygg" is one name) and to the legend that Yggdrasil was actually Woden's steed, the "seat" of his bottom.

[23] Here, stone is related to law and dogma which are equated with sin and death:

> —A shrub of libertine, indeed! But that steyne of
> law indead what stiles its neming?
> —Tod, tod [death], too hard parted! [ossified]　(505.
> 21–23).

²⁴ The Porters' daughter, Isobel, is called "child of tree" (556.19).

7] *Tea*

²⁵ Also see 432.6–7, 9, 11–12; 519.10–11; 581.1. One will recognize the Greek letters Phi and Theta, chosen to complete an alphabet of 28 rather than 26 letters.

²⁶ Cf. the Prankquean's wetting of the "dour." And, as Clive Hart says (*Structure and Motif*, pp. 206–8), micturition as an act of creation is identified with the wine of communion, as well as with "baptismal waters."

²⁷ E.g., 584.10–11 (after the last copulation of HCE and ALP) : "Three for two will do for me and he for thee and she for you"; 603.12–13: "shay for shee and sloo for slee"; 620.33: "He's for thee what she's for me."

²⁸ In my opinion, "Peg" derives from *pige,* the Danish word for "girl," and "Maggy," "Margaret," and "Peg" are simply variants of that term—Maggy being used when Joyce wants to connect the word with majesty: "that . . . variant *maggers* for the more generally accepted *majesty* which is but a trifle and yet may quietly amuse" (120.16–18). Cf. Glugg's "trifle" (223.22). ALP, consort of the teaparty king, is called "queen of teatable & W.C." Thomas E. Connolly, ed., *Scribbledehobble* (Evanston: Northwestern University Press, 1961), p. 27.

²⁹ Atherton has dug up from accounts in medical books the interesting information that the amount of male ejaculation is supposed to be one teaspoonful (*Books,* p. 154).

³⁰ Jaun, wishing he could begin again, with his mother's new golden egg, to travel downstream with the minnows, says: "but I'd turn back as lief as not if I could only spoonfind the nippy girl of my heart's appointment, Mona Vera Toutou Ipostila, my lady of Lyons [Lyons teahouses, London], to guide me by gastronomy under her safe conduct . . . I'd ask no kinder of the fates than to stay where I am, with my tinny of brownie's tea . . . leaving tealeaves for the trout, and belleeks for the wary" (449.9–34). Also cf. passage from HCE's self-justification: "I protest there is luttrelly not one teaspoonspill of evidence at bottomlie to my babad, as you shall see, as this is. Keemun Lapsang of first pickings" (534.9–11).

³¹ "And that salubrated sickenagiaour of yaours have teaspilled

all my hazeydency" (305.3–4). Sometimes the kind of "tea" that results only in dry sterility is distinguished as beeftea. (In *Ulysses,* too, beeftea serves as a euphemism for urine.) Issy, in one of her footnotes, says, "If I'd more in the cups that peeves thee [than beef tea] you could cracksmith your rows tureens" (304, n. 4). Cf. "Mawmaw, luk, your beeeftay's fizzin over" (308.R1) and "His Bouf Toe is Frozen Over" (in connection with a miscarriage of the "letter": 421.9).

32 See "low" Shem's preference for "tea-time salmon tinned" (170.26–27), and Shaun's fond memory of his "tinny of brownie's tea" (449.13). Another misuse of "teatime" is suggested in the twins' indulging in "tinned" or canned varieties of the "communion" elements; perhaps this refers to the sins of non-propagating adventures.

33 Hart, *Structure and Motif,* p. 199.

8] *The*

34 *Joyce-Agains Wake* (Seattle, 1965), p. 100.

35 *Ibid.,* pp. 112–13 (footnote). Also cf. p. 105: "Man replaces God in *Finnegans Wake,* and the cycles of life replace Christianity."

36 "With nought a wired from the wordless either" (223.34) is from the passage where Glugg seeks help from the four gospelers, from his mother, and then from the ass.

37 "And the chicks picked their teeths [the's] and the dombkey he begay began. You can ask your ass if he believes it" 20.25–26).

38 See Atherton, p. 31: "This attribution of Original Sin to God is one of the basic axioms of *Finnegans Wake.*"

39 "With acknowledgment of our fervour [father] of the first instant he remains years most fainfully [fane: temple, church; feign-fully]. For postscrapt see spoils" (124.30–32).

40 Also suggests Pythagorean and Platonic beliefs in the mystic qualities of geometry, which Joyce seems to share in his attention to geometric patterns for his god-man symbols.

41 "Scatter brand to the reneweller of the sky, thou who agnitest! Dah! Arcthuris comeing! Be! Verb umprincipiant through the trancitive spaces! Kilt by kelt shell kithagain with kinagain. We elect for thee, Tirtangel. Svadesia salve! We Durbalanars, theeadjure. . . . Now if soomone felched a twoel and soomonelses warmet watter we could . . . make sunlike sylp

om this warful dune's battam" (594.1–12). The references to "the," "om," and King Arthur should be noted.

[42] In conjunction with woman and tea, there can be detected signs of "a wick weak woking from ennemberable Ashias unto fierce force fuming, temtem tamtam, the Phoenican wakes" (608.30–32).

[43] In the "middenhide hoard of objects" turned up out of the past are "snake wurrums everyside!" Ireland, rid of snakes through St. Patrick, seems to have been rid of sex, as well, through Irish Catholicism. "They came to our island from triangular Toucheaterre beyond the wet prairie rared up in the midst of the cargon of prohibitive pomefructs but along landed Paddy Wippingham and the his garbagecans cotched the creeps of them pricker than our whosethere outofman could quick up her whatsthats" (19.12–18).

[44] One has to deal with perversion in respect to the whole concept of the T-deity, as will be shown in the chapter which follows. The sinner in the park, though legitimately assuming the names of "Atem" and "Om," is still bound to be aligned with "Tom" and anal sexual activity. "But, of course, he could call himself Tem, too, if he had time to? You butt he could anytom" (88.35–36).

3   KEY FIGURES

9] *Three, Two, and One*

[1] "Many . . . Tieckle . . . Forsin" alludes to the handwriting on the wall, interpreted by Daniel for King Nebuchadnezzar: "Mene, Mene, Tekel, Upharsin . . . Thy kingdom is divided, and given to the Medes and Persians" (Daniel 5: 25–28). Joyce's language adds: Many tickle for sin. Races interbreed. The handwriting on the wall says that your kingdom must be given over to your maids and poor sons.

[2] *A Concordance to Finnegans Wake.* (Minneapolis: University of Minnesota Press, 1963).

[3] The count for two is higher, since it is the number for the male twins as well as for the female genitalia-temptresses. The twins function alone part of the time—not always in connection with the central figure.

[4] "Long Lally Tobkids . . . swore like a Norewheezian tailliur on the stand . . . that he was up against a right querrshnorrt of

a mand in the butcher of the blues who, he guntinued, on last epening . . . went and . . . hickicked at the dun and dorass [stirrup cup (deoch an dorass) ; door of ass] against all the runes and, when challenged about the pretended hick (it was kickup and down with him) . . . said simply: I appop pie oath [I apologize; upon my oath], Phillyps Captain. . . . And Phelps was flayful with his peeler [playful with his feeler]. But his phizz fell" (67.11–27). The opposition of two and three, elsewhere, is referred to as "two sisters of charities on the front steps and three evacuan cleansers at the back gaze [gate]" (362.25–26). In one account given by the "privates," Sockerson and Jimmy and Fred (Freda) , "he puts his feeler to me behind the beggar's bush, does Freda" (588.1–2) .

5 Shakespeare's alleged relationship with Mister W.H. is also referred to several times in hidden allusions. In a passage on FW 143, which contains many echos of *Hamlet,* there is a reference to "ingredient and egregiunt *w*hights and ways to *w*hich in the curse of his persistence the course of his story *will* had been having recourses" (143.10–12; italics mine) .

6 "Same capman no nothing horces two feller [queer] he feller go where." But when "three newcommers till knockingshop at the ones upon a topers," there is "admittance to that impedance" (322.25–28) .

7 A "free" translation: "Eeny meeny miney mo, free is woman and sweet is she too, three is too (free; to two) when love is free, wicked anna woe is we! A pair of sycophants in panties with almond-shaped (magdelen) eyes, one old lobster (humpty dumpty) and three meddlers on the sly." For mathematicians more patient than I, here is another set of equations which ought to provide hours of entertainment, since possible combinations defy a single translation: "Axe [x] on thwacks on thracks, axenwise [axlewise]. One by one place one be three dittoh and one before. Two nursus one make a plausible free and idim behind" (19.20–22) . For a start, "by" = next to, "times," two; "place" = please, add to; "be" = equals, by; "dittoh" = same as before, two; "before" = "equals four," in front of; "nursus" = nurseys, minus; "make" = equals, is successful sexually; "free" = three, tree; "idim" = "a dim," item (one) , Atem, idem (ditto) . Etcetera.

8 The passages above are taken from 365.27–366.33. The last sentence connects the homosexual encounter in the park with both the Russian-general story and the captain-and-tailor story (whole suit of clothes) .

⁹ For further confirmation of the nature of the incidents in the park, see 86.14–15: The "King," disguised, went to "the middle-white fair" "ellegedly with a pedigree pig [*pige* (girl)] . . . and a hyacinth [for discussion of "hyacinth" as homosexually significant, see part 1]; 134.36–135.4 (adds reference to the waiting "queen") : "the king was in his cornerwall [Cornwall] melking mark so murry, the queen was steep in armbour feeling fain and furry, the mayds was midst the hawthorns shoeing up their hose, out pimps the back guards (pomp!) and pump gun they goes"; 138.13–14 (combines park episode with Buckley perversion) : "was waylaid of a parker [*pige* in park] and beschotten by a buckeley"; 340.22–24: "For he devoused [defiled; devoured; divorced] the lelias on the fined [lilies of the field] and he conforted [consorted with; comforted] samp, tramp and marchint [the three] out of the drumbume of a narse [jawbone of an ass; bum . . . "arse"]"; "Limbers affront of him, lumbers [soldiers; "trees"] behund" (339.7) ; "This is his largos life, this is me timtomtum and this is her two peekweeny ones" (519.10–11). Also see perversion hints regarding Russian general in 338.24–27 and 343.22–25.

¹⁰ The three lipoleums are described as "an inimyskilling inglis," "a scotcher grey" and "a davy"—or a "Welsh one" (Joyce's first draft). The Welsh one, later called "me Belchum," is the center fellow who sneaks his "phillippy" out, and the two "bag" lipoleums, on each side, are said to be "mordering" each other. The confusion cannot be entirely cleared up, because "me Belchum" is, after all, not really an entity separate from the Willingdone.

¹¹ ALP, the mother, is definitely connoted here, with her two mounts of Venus. "Grand Mons Injun" refers to the grand man's "engine" more than to St. John. ALP is apparently ready to shelter her three men, but the tempting jinnies provoke a war. It is not yet time for the mother-to-the-rescue act.

¹² "To all his foretellers he reared a stone and for all his comethers he planted a tree" (135.4–5) ; "he crashed in the hollow of the park, trees down, as he soared in the vaguum of the phoenix, stones up" (136.33–35) .

10] Plain Geometry

¹³ *Structure and Motif*, p. 45.
¹⁴ Refers to the dividing quality of the "pole" as from the corner of a graph.

15 Among items included in this word are: P and T; the windows; one door; one and x; circle (s) ; close up; and the beginning and ending "p's" as the "two."

16"If this habby cyclic erdor be outraciously enviolated by a mierelin roundtableturning, like knuts in maze, the zitas [z's; cities; *situs* (Latin) : position] runnind hare and dart with the yeggs in their muddle, like a seven of wingless arrows, hodge-padge, thump, kick and hurry, . . . while the catched and dodged exarx [XRX; eggs; arcs] seems himmulteemiously to beem . . . the ersed [arsed; first] ladest mand and . . . the losed farce on erroroots [allusion to Noah on Ararat?] . . . мРм brings us a rainborne pamtomomiom. . . . Binomeans to be comprendered. Inexcessible as thy by god ways [the bygone days]" (285.1–29) . In this passage, mixed-up sex adds to the pandemonium ("hend" and "tail," "ersed," "ladest mand," numbers that don't add up) which includes such opposites as a flood destroying the universe and a sere, evening world.

17 Hart, *Structure and Motif*, p. 62.

18 *Letters,* p. 252, n. 1.

19 I believe A. Walton Litz was the first to point this out, in *The Art of James Joyce* (London, 1961) , p. 117*n.*

20 Dolph's language connotes micturition and water all the way through the lesson: "tew tricklesome poinds" includes, among other things, "dew," "trickles," and "ponds"; "doubleviewed seeds" can be read as "W. C." (watercloset) ; there are references to mud, to water in a bucket *("aqua in buccat")* and to the river —"flument, fluvey and fluteous, midden wedge of the stream's your muddy old triagonal delta . . . the constant of fluxion, Mahame-wetma" (297.22–30) .

21 A reference to Lewis Carroll's Alice and her looking-glass world is also included, when Dolph describes his mathematical proposition as "One of the most *murmur*able *loose caroll*aries ever *Ellis threw his cookingclass*" (294.7–8; italics mine) .

22 The word "accomplasses" not only suggests furtive activity of accomplices (both male and female, for "lasses" are in "ac-complasses") but also connotes the North-South, East-West opposition of the twins' "orbits." Cf. Hart's figure III (*Structure and Motif,* p. 117) , and discussion of the two-dimensional flattening of the sphere, below. Also see the instruction to "tetraturn a somersault" for the drawing of the second circle, a probable allusion to the four points of the compass.

23 To facilitate explication, I have supplied the quotation marks which Joyce left out, so that it can be seen which twin says what. At first it would seem that "Ay, I'm right here, Nickel, and I'll write" must be Dolph, referring to himself as "Nickel," since he is the one associated with art and writing; however, Mick has his "exegesis" to write, and he is in the "right."

24 "Balked his bawd of parodies" also alludes to Joyce as the writer of parodies, and connects him with the non-angelic twin.

25 I am using the translation by Francis M. Cornford (New York, 1959). For much of which follows, I am deeply indebted to Clive Hart, *Structure and Motif*—especially his discussion of Joyce's use of *Timaeus* on pages 129–34, and the illustration of the "orbits" of the twins on page 117.

26 The Same and the Other occasionally refer, in *Finnegans Wake,* to hetero- and homosexuality, as well as to the twins in their other opposing aspects: "About *that* and the *other*. If he was not alluding to the *whole in the wall*? That he was when he was not eluding from the *whole of the woman*" (90.21–23; italics mine).

27 *Structure and Motif*, p. 130.

28 P. D. Ouspensky, *A New Model of the Universe* (New York, 1943), p. 373.

29 Cf. *Timaeus,* p. 56: "For ourselves . . . we postulate as the best of these many triangles one kind, passing over all the rest; that, namely, a pair of which compose the equilateral triangle."

30 See 462.19–20, regarding "Dave the Dancekerl": "could he quit doubling and stop tippling, he would be the unicorn of his kind. He's the mightiest penumbrella I ever flourished on behond the shadow of a post!" The passage conveys ghost-like, shadowy connotations—again hinting at a mysterious mirror world, to be dealt with below. It also carries biographical suggestions of the Joyce-Shem identification; this inferior member of the Trinity is a *pen*umbrella, a mere shadow of the "family umbroglia," the "Tullagrovepole."

31 Cf. Shaun as a barrel in Book III.

32 Variations of this shape are suggested in "simpletop," "papacocopotl" (294.24; papa volcano, "Popocatepetl"), "cyclone" (294.10), and "gyre" ("Gyre O, gyre O, gyrotundo!": 295.23–24).

33 In Tarot symbolism, the triangle represents the noumenal (objective) world, the square represents the phenomenal (subjective) world, and the dot, placed in the center of the triangle

within the square—or of the square within the triangle—stands for man (Ouspensky, *A New Model,* pp. 187–88). When the "two" and the "three" comprise a quincunx, the center dot, as the penis, is in the proper position as the "man" within the composite sexual universe.

34 Shem as Dave the Dancekerl comes to take Shaun's place "on quinquisecular cycles after his French evolution" (462.34). Also see 567.33, regarding "bikeygels and troykakyls [troika-karls; tricycles] and those puny farting little solitires" (solitaires, in reference to the perverted three-plus-one, but also solar tires, suggesting a ride in space, like stars in a constellation formation).

35 See the "fiveaxled production, *The Coach With The Six In-sides*" (359.23–24). In the context of the geometry lesson, we have the sentence, "I bring town eau and curry nothung up my sleeve" (295.17–18), which includes (as well as "I bring down O" and "I bring the town water") implications of "tonneau" and "surrey."

11] *The Coach with the Sex Insides*

36 See Robert Bierman's provocative discussion of this idea and its relevance to time and space in *Finnegans Wake*: "*Ulysses* and *Finnegans Wake*: the Explicit, the Implicit, and the Tertium Quid," *Renascence,* XI (Autumn 1958), 14–19.

37 In the role of Noah-God, the father "scooped the hens, hounds and horses biddy by bunny, with an arc of his covethand [ark of the covenant; rainbow; also, "within the ark"], saved from the drohnings they might oncounter, untill [into] his cubid long [cube; (300) cubits long: dimension of Noah's ark, Gen. 6:15], to hide in dry. Aside [*drei-zwei* (three-two); dry inside]" (321.26–29).

38 Sometimes the coach is drawn by horses on the ground. The last things HCE claims he did for his "Livvy" were: to wall in the things he had "built" for her—cities, gardens, churches, sons and daughters—to plant columns ("circulums") at several directions ("nordsoud," "eastmoreland and westlandmore"), and map out boulevards; then, to get the whole thing in motion like a hearse ("hearsemen, opslo!"), a train (with a "cundoctor"), a car ("vongn"), a coach with horses ("arabinstreeds"), a rickshaw, a shay, a taxi, a sedan. Then, "my damsells softsidesaddled, covertly, covertly, and Lawdy Dawe a perch behind: the mule and

the hinny and the jennet and the mustard nag and piebald shjelties and skewbald awknees steppit lively . . . for her pleashadure" (553.18–554.7) .

[39] Now the person assailed seems to be the "female" partner in the homosexual event, for "she" is the ondt ("aunt") in the ondt-gracehoper opposition.

[40] See 60.11–12: "Brian Lynsky, the *cub* curser, was questioned at his shouting *box*" (italics mine) ; 104.14: One of the names for the "letter" is "Rebus de Hibernicis"—meaning a pictorial representation of the word-elements in "Hibernicis" (hibernating bear; also Ireland, or "Hibernia") .

[41] The four gospelers, in this particular image, appear to be the four stars constituting the handle of the Big Dipper. See "old doxologers, in the suburrs of [suburbs of; sub-Ursa (i.e., the tail of Ursa)] the heavenly gardens" (454.30) ; also see reference to "coach and four" (143.1). Matthew is apparently the corner star and John is the tail-end of the handle. "First Murkiss, or so they sankeyed. Dodo! O Clearly! And Gregorio at front with Johannes far in back. Aw, aw!" (533.20–22) .

[42] Cf. "cubical" reference in 384.20–28: "he was kiddling and cuddling and bunnyhugging scrumptious his colleen bawn and dinkum belle, an oscar sister, on the fifteen inch loveseat, behind the chieftaness stewardesses, *cub*in, the hero . . . vicemversem her ragbags et assaucyetiams, *fore and aft, on and offsides* . . . whisping and lisping her about Trisolanisans, how one was whips for one was two and two was lips for one was three." (Italics mine.) Also cf. 385.36–386.3, which places the four old voyeurs outside the cube looking in through a peephole, able to see, but not to hear: "Lady, it was just too gorgeous, that expense of a lovely tint, embellished by the charms of art and very well conducted and nicely mannered and all the horrid rudy noises locked up in nasty cubbyhole!"

[43] Jaun says to "Sis" that he'd rather "stay where I am, with my tinny of brownie's tea [tin box of T], under the invocation [invitation] of Saint Jamas Hanway [Shem] . . . and Jacobus a Pershawm [Shem for Shaun], intercissous [interincestuous], for my thurifex [thurifer—one who carries the thurible; thorough satisfaction; effects], with Peter Roche [stone (homosexuality)], that frind of my boozum, leaning on my *cub*its . . . where I'll dreamt that I'll dwealth *mid* warblers' *walls*" (449.13–19; italics mine) .

44 It will be seen that the first three blocks resemble the letters, H C E.

45 "Madges Tighe" (majesty) is always waiting and "hoping to Michal" for this side of the cube to "turn up" with its "cupital tea before her ephumeral comes off without any much father which is parting *parcel* [box] of the same goumeral's postoppage, it being lookwhyse on the whence blows weather helping mickle so that the *loiter end* of that leader may *t*waddle out after a *cub*ital lull with a hopes soon to ear, comprong?" (369.30–370.1; italics mine).

46 Cf. astronomical and cubical suggestions in 194.12–20: "it is to you, firstborn and firstfruit of woe [Abel], to me, branded sheep [Cain], pick of the wasterpaperbaskel . . . you alone, wind-blasted tree of the knowledge of beautiful andevil, ay, clothed upon with the *metuor* and shimmering like the *horescens, astroglodynamonologos,* the child of Nilfit's father, blzb [Illfit and Beelzebub refer to the Cain twin who is of the same father as the Abel twin], to me unseen blusher in an obscene coalhole, the *cubilibum* of your secret sigh [the equilibrium of your secret side; "bum" of the opposite side of the cube], dweller in the downandoutermost where voice only of the dead may come" (italics mine).

47 "I recknitz wharfore the darling murrayed her mirror. She did? Mersey me!" (208.35–36).

48 The perplexing suggestion in the word "nonplussing" is that his "length by breadth" is *no more than* his thickness.

49 "And it is what they began to say to him tetrahedrally then, the masters, what way was he" (477.1–2). They are going to fish for him with their "quadriliberal" nets, as if he were in a spatial sea (477.19–20).

50 Hart alludes to "the new world of physics of which Joyce was trying to build up a faithful verbal analogue" (*Structure and Motif,* p. 65), in his discussion of the "Secret Cycle" of *Finnegans Wake.* Joyce refers to Einstein's work as "the whoo-whoo and where's hairs theorics of Winestain" (149.27–28).

51 The "letter" is, at one point, called "Anna Stessa's Rise to Notice" (104.8): Anna's Tessa's (tesseract's) erection.

52 All kinds of literature of the new physics, which discussed the geometrical possibilities of the fourth dimension, were available to Joyce. Some of those which carried non-mathematical implications are: Henry P. Manning, ed., *The Fourth Dimension Simply Explained* (a series of essays submitted to *Scientific American*

in 1908 on the subject of the fourth dimension), New York: Munn and Company, 1910; Henry P. Manning, *Geometry of Four Dimensions*, New York, 1914 (a drawing of the tesseract-cross appears on p. 240); Charles W. R. Hooker, *What is the Fourth Dimension?*, London, 1934; Edwin A. Abbott, *Flatland* (I have not been able to discover the date this science-fiction classic was first published, but the "Second and Revised Edition" came out in 1884, probably in London. It is now in its seventh edition and is published by Dover Publications, Inc., New York, 1952); P. D. Ouspensky, *Tertium Organum*, translated from the Russian by Nicholas Bessaraboff and Claude Bragdon, New York, 1934 (12th printing; translation first published 1920 by Manas Press, Rochester); Ouspensky, *A New Model of the Universe* (first published 1931), cited earlier in this work. I have depended a great deal on Ouspensky, since his approach to the new science is one of application to religion, art, and especially the occult. Joyce "romanticizes" scientific concepts in an analogous way.

For the drawings of the unfolded cube (p. 116), and information in general about the four-dimensional tesseract, I have drawn from Martin Gardner, "Mathematical Games," in the November, 1966, issue of *Scientific American* (pp. 138–43).

[53] Ouspensky (*A New Model*, p. 126) refers to a drawing of "the perfect man," by J. G. Gichtel, a seventeenth-century mystic, in which the lower part of the body with its sexual organs is called "Monde Tenebreux," and is said to contain the "Root of Souls in the Centre of the Universe." And Gichtel's comments were that "man has become so earthly and outward . . . that he seeks afar, beyond the starry sky, in the higher eternity, what is quite near him, within the inner centre of his soul."

[54] For confrontations between these two factions, see 188.14–25 and 190.33–191.4. In addition, the entire Mookse and Gripes story (pp. 152–5) can be read to illustrate the antagonism.

[55] Ouspensky, *A New Model*, p. 106.

[56] Gazebo: the structure from which the extensive prospect is viewed; crotonic acid; a compound used in organic synthesis; stereopticon: the projector through which two pictures of the same object blend. Here, "tetradomational" refers to the four gazers (four-dimensional creatures?), the "Mamma Lujah."

[57] Suggestive of sundry dissipated elements being sent through the mail-male; also of sun-son dance.

[58] Anastomosis: communication through blood vessels by means of collateral channels; also "mosaically": fitting pieces together to form a whole design.

[59] Both "preter-" and "para-" are prefixes for "beyond" (cf. "preterhuman": beyond what is human); "paradisaically" and "idiotically" are also connoted.

[60] Shits pen to paper; wets his shitting pen; is pa-pee-er for his "pen."

[61] Ouspensky, *A New Model*, p. 378.

[62] Pointland is one of the worlds described in Abbott, *Flatland*, pp. 93–95: "The point . . . is himself his own World, his own Universe. . . . There arose from the little buzzing creature a tiny, low, monotonous but distinct tinkling . . . from which I caught these words, "Infinite beatitude of existence! It is; and there is none else beside It. . . . it is the One, and yet the All in All. Ah, the happiness, ah, the happiness of Being!"

INDEX

Abel, 17, 137n30, 153n46
Adam, 4, 14, 30, 74, 97, 107, 126
Alice (Lewis Carroll character), 18, 60, 102, 122, 149n21
ALP: analogies and variants, 5, 16–18, 36, 39, 53, 63, 105, 106, 107, 126, 135n16, 153n51; dualistic aspects of, 13, 18, 19–20, 92, 106; last coition with HCE, 15, 53, 78, 144n27; her majesty, 18, 144n28; her comments on major themes, 42, 86–87, 88, 122; symbolic associations, 50, 63, 90, 99, 101, 138n35, 142n4, 148n11; mentioned, 64, 65, 134–35n15
Alphabet symbolism: P, 17, 19–20, 55, 56, 77, 89, 107, 149n15; Q, 19–20, 55; X, 63, 68, 79, 93, 127, 147n7, 149n15, 149n16; E, 105, 110, 117–18
Ann, Anna, Anna Livia Plurabelle. See ALP
Antonius, 61
Arc de Triomphe, 10, 50, 134n11
Armor, 11, 16, 17, 134n14
Art, viii, 12, 24, 106, 119, 125, 128, 141n58, 154n54
Arthur, King, 11, 84, 92, 137n29, 145–46n41
Ass, 23, 62, 72, 82, 116, 145n36, 145n37, 147n4, 148n9
Atem, 48, 146n44, 147n7

Baptism, 9, 15, 20, 39, 57, 80, 139n45, 144n26
Bear, 114–15, 152n40
Berkeley, George. See Shem
Bible, the, 3, 81, 100, 111
Big Dipper. See Ursa Major
Bloom, Leopold, vii, viii
Bloom, Molly, vii, 67
Book of Kells, 62–64, 82, 141n2, 142n7. See also Tunc page
Book of the Dead, 64
Bride, Julia, 143n20
Bride-ship, 113, 123, 152n42
Bridge, 41, 50–51
Bruno, Giordano, 12
Buckley. See Shem
Burrus, 61
Butt. See Twins

Cad, the, 31, 40, 114–15, 140n51, 141n54
Cain, 17, 153n46
Carroll, Lewis, 18, 149n21
Caseous, 61
Castration, 46–47, 54, 56
Christ, Jesus, 61–62, 73, 75, 80, 81, 82, 83, 86, 107, 143n20
Chuff. See Shaun
Claudius, King, 45
Claybook, 4, 89
Clothes, 12–13, 40, 41, 42, 53, 55–56, 57, 140n54
Cole, Kitty, 78
Constellation, 113, 114–15, 116,